THE
GRUNT
PADRE

FATHER VINCENT ROBERT CAPODANNO
VIETNAM 1966-1967

BY

REV. DANIEL L. MODE

The Grunt Padre:
Father Vincent Robert Capodanno
Vietnam 1966–1967
by Rev. Daniel L. Mode

Softcover: ISBN # 1-891280-08-2
Hardcover: ISBN # 1-891280-17-1

Library of Congress Catalog Card Number # 99-069490

2nd Printing with additions 5/01.

Publisher:
CMJ Marian Publishers
Post Office Box 661
Oak Lawn, Illinois 60454
www.cmjbooks.com
jwby@aol.com

Marketing Agent:
Hartnett Incorporated
4209 South 35th Street
Arlington, Virginia 22206
hartnettinc@mindspring.com

Graphics:
Michelle Winkler

Manufactured in the United States of America

DEDICATION

To

All Military Chaplains Who Gave Their Lives

"A martyrdom is always the design of God, for His love of men, to warn them and to lead them, to bring them back to His ways. It is never the design of man; for the true martyr is he who has become the instrument of God, who has lost his will in the will of God...."

T.S. Eliot, *Murder in the Cathedral*

And

To

Captain Paul J. Mode, USN

My father who showed me the Navy and shared with me the Faith.

TABLE OF CONTENTS

FOREWORD

The Grunt Padre is the story of Father Vincent Capodanno, a Maryknoll missionary, who left his small Taiwanese parish to support the fine men and women of the United States Marine Corps where they faced the threat of death on the most forward edge of the firing lines in a distant Asian country called South Vietnam. That is how I met and came to know Father Vince.

Leaving Taiwan, Father Vincent became a Navy chaplain and ultimately was assigned to a United States Marine Corps Infantry Regiment. As a chaplain, a man of God, he had no command authority like other officers. Yet he inspired a loyalty surpassing that of the finest officers because of the individual he was, because of the special love and kindness he offered us, and because of his willingness to share the hardships of the most junior Marines. Father Vince became one of the most known and most respected men "in country." He became the "Grunt Padre" to the warfighters.

Assigned to a regiment which spread over twenty-five miles, each day was a day of travel as the chaplain made his weekly rounds of fifteen or twenty different companies. He quietly pursued his mission, caring for the spiritual needs of all Marines. He was ecumenical and accepted by all as their chaplain. The Marines knew which day was their day with Father Vincent, and, like people waiting for the postman to bring a special letter, the Grunt Marines looked forward to seeing Father Vincent appear along the trail leading to their positions. Once there, Father Vincent made the rounds, talking with as many weary warriors as possible. Mass was held; general absolution was given to all. All faiths attended his services. Marines came in their battle gear, fresh from night patrols, postponing sleep, for Father Vincent was there to share a few moments with them. He listened to them, offering each infantryman individual care and attention. He understood them. As nightfall approached its grave dangers approached, Father Vincent quickly moved on to the next unit.

This chaplain did not recoil from danger. As his Marines assembled for combat operations, he would be there. He crowded into any available helicopter space and flew into the "hot landing zones" to be available to Marines facing combat. Father Vince carried no rifle. He carried a cross — a man of peace carrying God's message to distant battlefields. During firefights, all the infantrymen watched over him, because they knew Father Vincent would otherwise move forward with complete disregard for his own life to render aid to any wounded or dying Marine. The unspoken word was "watch over our Padre." On September 4, 1967, Father Vincent Capodanno gallantly gave his life attempting to rescue a wounded corpsman. As an officer in his regiment, I can personally attest to the fact that the news of his death had a more devastating impact upon the morale of the whole 1st Marine Division than the loss of many other senior combat leaders. We loved the Padre who so loved us.

As fate would have it, a young seminarian, Daniel Lawrence Mode, began a research paper on Father Vincent decades after the Grunt Padre's death. Later, as an ordained priest, Father Mode continued his research, interviewing nearly one hundred individuals to discover the whole story behind this man of God and his personal commitment to serve his Creator in any time or place.

Father Mode's book is more than a story of a fallen hero; his writing builds a mosaic. His meticulous research and discoveries have enabled him to paint a picture of a special man before the colors of time begin to fade on Father Vincent's life, on his commitment to God, on his love for his fellow man, and on his unselfish sacrifices. *The Grunt Padre* reminds us that one man can make a difference in the lives of many. In completing this book, Father Mode offers a lasting contribution to the historic legacy of the Navy Chaplain Corps as well. His book is a wonderful read for men and women of all faiths and walks of life.

Colonel Gerald H. Turley
United States Marine Corps (Retired)
Author of *The Easter Offensive: Vietnam 1972*

PREFACE

I first learned of Father Vincent Robert Capodanno during the summer of 1989. At that time, I was a Navy Chaplain Candidate at the Chaplains School in Newport, Rhode Island. Having heard a brief account of his death in Vietnam, I was impressed by Father Vincent's heroic sacrifice. I believed that in a small way I could identify with this chaplain who died in 1967, six months after I was born. Like my classmates at the Chaplains School, I had a great desire to be a priest and to serve as a Navy chaplain.

While I was studying at Mount Saint Mary's Seminary in Emmitsburg, Maryland, and casting about for an M.A. research paper, Father Vincent emerged as a likely subject. Initially, I was going to opt for a fifty-page paper in which I would review the most publicly known events of his life. But the more I discovered about this remarkable man, the more I realized that such a modest paper would not do justice to him and to the ideals for which he stood. I wanted to determine the "whys" behind his actions, including the motivation for his joining the Chaplain Corps and his going to Vietnam with the U.S. Marines. I wanted to do as thorough a study as possible of this dedicated and brave priest. Consequently, I wrote a lengthy thesis rather than a brief paper.

When I began my research, I was amazed to discover the lack of readily available information on Father Vincent. I was able to find a few published articles, yet nothing that thoroughly explained his life. Despite the scarcity of public information, I was fortunate in locating his church and Navy records, and subsequently collected hundreds of documents related to almost every aspect of his short life. Most importantly, I established contact with over fifty people who knew Father Vincent as a family member, missionary or chaplain, and who were willing to share with me their accounts of his life as it touched theirs.

Shortly after beginning my research, I realized that Father Vincent's story also constituted a significant piece of American military history. In particular, I believed it was a missing page in the annals of the Vietnam War. I reflected on that war which has received so much attention on the screen and in literature, but whose heroes have been given far too little notice. I came to appreciate one of those heroes, Father Vincent Capodanno, who inspired many Marines to serve beyond the call of duty, and who challenged military chaplains and others to seek God through serving others.

The last hours of Father Vincent's life make up the most public and valiant period of his time in Vietnam and merit special attention. Therefore, I have detailed accounts of those last critical forty-eight hours of his life.

It should also be noted that, in presenting material on Father Vincent's priestly formation, I have highlighted some of the history and traditions of the Catholic Foreign Mission Society of America, popularly known as Maryknoll, the religious society to which Father Vincent belonged. I have also given an overview of the history of the U.S. Chaplain Corps. In order to understand properly the motive behind Father Vincent's heroic actions, his deeds must be understood in light of those who preceded him in both Maryknoll and the Chaplain Corps. Father Vincent would have been the first to point out that any glory attributed to him was supported and reflected in the sacrifice of many others. Therefore, I have presented brief accounts of the lives of some of these courageous individuals who may have been an influence in Father Vincent's own valiant life.

I also have included information on the many memorials that have been dedicated to Father Vincent Capodanno. These, and others yet to come, show that Father Vincent is far from being a forgotten hero of the past.

Finally, in my research I was introduced to a wonderful little book, *Radiating Christ: An Appeal to Militant Catholics*, written in 1944 by a Jesuit priest, Father Raoul Plus. This work was familiar to Father Vincent and other Maryknoll priests. I was struck by how closely Father Vincent's career paralleled the four stages of the spiritual life that Father Plus posits. These stages — Descent, Incarnation, Renunciation and Burial — are the basis for the chapters concerned with Father Vincent's adult life.

During the past decade, I have met hundreds of people who knew Father Vincent. Many asked for copies of my thesis, which was initially distributed in 1992, and others encouraged me to publish it as a book. This work expands on my earlier research and brings the Capodanno story up to date. It is a story that needs to be told on behalf of veterans and chaplains, and for the benefit of all those who cherish the ideals of commitment and sacrifice.

Rev. Daniel L. Mode
Falls Church, Virginia
October 1999

ACKNOWLEDGEMENTS

I would like to thank some of the many people who assisted me in the preparation of this book, which started as a thesis at Mount Saint Mary's Seminary. At Mount Saint Mary's, they include Sister Ann Miriam Gallagher, R.S.M., who served as my director and first reader; Rev. Michael J. Roach, my second reader; Sister Joan Gormley, S.S.M.W., who provided critical and editorial assistance; Professor T. Kelly Fitzpatrick, who contributed material support; Rev. Mr. Leo Kosch, who printed the second edition; and Rev. Msgr. Kenneth W. Roeltgen, Seminary Rector, who offered much encouragement.

Apart from the Mount Saint Mary's Community, sincere gratitude is extended to the many people who allowed me to interview them and publish some of their memories, most notably, Mrs. Gloria Holman, Mr. James Capodanno, and the late Mrs. Pauline Costa.

Also to be recognized are representatives of major organizations with whom I collaborated to ensure I had the necessary documentation. Among them are William Taylor of the Chaplain Resource Board, Norfolk, Virginia; Robert Aquilina of the Marine Corps Historical Foundation, Washington, D.C.; Rev. John F. Harrington, M.M. of the Catholic Foreign Mission Society of America, Maryknoll, New York; and Mrs. Danna Rae Hardy of Vietnam Awareness, Inc., Toledo, Ohio.

I especially acknowledge and extend a sincere thank you to Mrs. Emma Eaton and Mrs. Teresa Purcell who volunteered their time and energy in countless ways, including editorial and secretarial assistance. Further, Mrs. Eaton almost miraculously organized and recorded the hundreds of documents used in the thesis.

Finally, my thanks to those instrumental in publishing this book, Teresa Hartnett of Arlington, Virginia, and James Gilboy, president of CMJ Marian Publishers of Oak Lawn, Illinois; as well as to those whose editorial assistance contributed to the final book, Joseph Esposito of Springfield, Virginia and Cynthia Nicolosi of the Fraternity of Mary Immaculate Queen, Bois le Roi, France.

INTRODUCTION

As the world passes into a new historical era, it cannot forget the disasters of the century just finished. But will it learn from them?

Ours has been called the bloodiest century ever known and the world's unrest continues even after the disintegration of Communist power. Local tyrants in increasing numbers are striving for nuclear parity with the United States which, as the undoubted and unchallenged world power, finds its military deployed in more parts of the world than ever before.

Thanks to the remarkable witness of Pope John Paul II and the results his courageous witness has brought about, the Catholic Church's worldwide prestige as a voice of moral leadership has never been greater. "Peace" is the constant call of the Holy See in all its diplomatic initiatives — peace founded on true freedom.

Why then is that same Holy See responsible for the appointment of thirty-five bishops whose pastoral responsibility it is to care for the spiritual needs of those nations which, in one fashion or other, encourage priest-chaplains to accompany their troops wherever they are sent. Two underlying principles in this regard are essential to appreciate.

First, the Church does not condemn standing armies of any nation — if their purpose is legitimate self-defense. And it holds in esteem those who serve their country in such a spirit. In the words of the Second Vatican Council:

> All those who enter the military services in loyalty to their country should look upon themselves as the custodians of the security and freedom of their fellow countrymen and when they carry out their duty properly, they are contributing to the maintenance of peace. (Church in the Modern World, #79)

A second principle is recognized by the Church and most nations and is a corollary to the above: No one should be deprived of, or forfeit, appropriate pastoral care because he or she has chosen a life of service to country. Therefore, in our American system, in spite of the many strictures forbidding the state's direct involvement in religion, the federal government salaries chaplains, builds churches, pays for classrooms and texts for religious instruction, among other things.

Do dangers lurk in this unusual marriage of church and state or, more specifically, of chaplain and military commander? Undoubtedly so. But to experience the system in actual operation, and especially through the prism of our chaplains' active ministry, is to demonstrate the extraordinary gift that the military chaplaincy is to both church and state.

Father Daniel Mode has done just this in his inspiring story of Maryknoll Father Vincent Robert Capodanno, the Grunt Padre. Father Capodanno was killed in the midst of a fierce battle between 500 American Marines and 2500 North Vietnamese Army regulars. A non-combatant, with no other protection than his deep priestly faith, he was wounded three times as he sought to give spiritual comfort to those who saw him as their Father and Pastor. He died on the battlefield and was later awarded the highest of all decorations, the Congressional Medal of Honor.

As riveting as Father Mode's description of those last two days of Father Capodannos life is, so much depth would be missing had not our author, with his own priestly sensitivity and insights, caringly and carefully traced the life of this American hero from his youthful days on Staten Island, through seminary and early priesthood. More than 100 individuals who knew Father Capodanno personally knew interviewed.

Here is a priest-chaplain who gave his life fully that others might know the love of God in the presence of Christ. Our thanks must be paid to Father Mode for bringing this holy life to light. May it inspire more future Father Capodanno's to attempt such self-giving!

Most Reverend Edwin F. O'Brien
Archbishop for the Military, U.S.A.

Over here [Vietnam] there is a written policy that if you get three Purple Hearts you go home within 48 hours. On Labor Day our battalion ran into a world of trouble — when Fr. C.[Capodanno] arrived on the scene it was 500 Marines against 2500 North Vietnamese Army regulars.

Needless to say, we were constantly on the verge of [being] completely overrun and the Marines on several occasions had to 'advance in a retrograde movement.' This left the dead and wounded outside the perimeter as the Marines slowly withdrew.

Casualties were running high and Fr. C. had his work cut out for him. Early in the day, he was shot through the right hand which all but shattered his hand — one corpsman patched him up and tried to med evac him but Fr. C. declined saying he had work to do.

A few hours later a mortar landed near him and left his right arm in shreds hanging from his side. Once again he was patched up and once again he refused evacuation. There he was, moving slowly from wounded to dead to wounded using his left arm to support his right as he gave absolution or last rites, when he suddenly spied a corpsman get knocked down by the burst of an automatic weapon.

The corpsman was shot in the leg and couldn't move and understandably panicked. Fr. C. ran out to him and positioned himself between the injured boy and the automatic weapon. Suddenly, the weapon opened up again and this time riddled Fr. C. from the back of his head to the base of his spine — and with his third Purple Heart of the day — Fr. C. went Home.

Lieutenant Joseph E. Pilon, M.D.
Christmas 1967

MEDAL OF HONOR
LT Vincent R. Capodanno, USNR
NAVY CHAPLAIN

AN ITALIAN-AMERICAN FAMILY

He summoned the crowd with his disciples and said to them, 'Whoever wishes to come after me must deny himself, take up his cross, and follow me. For whoever wishes to save his life will lose it; and whoever loses his life for my sake and that of the gospel will save it.'

(Mark 8:34–35)

In the town square of Gaeta, Italy, above the shining waters of the Mediterranean Sea, stands a memorial to an American Navy chaplain. The remarkable story of Father Vincent Capodanno begins here, among ordinary people whose faith and courage carried them to a new life in a new land. When Vincent Capodanno, Sr. left Italy in 1901, he could hardly have imagined that eighty-nine years after his departure, a sculpture in memory of his son — his namesake — would grace the center of his native place. Yet, such was the pride of a family whose strong ties endured across generations and evolving world events.

The Italian name Capodanno means literally "head of the year," or "New Year." With all the high expectations that the term implies, sixteen-year-old Vincent Capodanno, Sr., arrived in the thriving harbor of New York City. The journey across the Atlantic had been long and arduous, and he knew greater challenges lay before him. Still, he could not help a thrill of excitement as he caught his first glimpse of his new country under the welcoming torch of the Statue of Liberty, a timeless symbol of hope and promise. Like millions of others, he was processed on Ellis Island and then released to make his way in a new land.

Italian immigration to the United States came in two waves. The first lasted from colonial times until shortly before the Civil War and consisted of middle class Italians largely from Northern Italy, who were, for the most part, skilled tradesmen and, in some cases, quite educated. They were motivated by a desire for freedom and the spirit of adventure.

Vincent Capodanno, Sr. was part of the second wave lasting from around 1880 until, more or less, the quota system of the 1924 Immigration Act. Between 1900 and World War I, an average of 200,000 Italians immigrated annually to America. By the time the quotas were put in place, an estimated 5,000,000 Italians were residing in the United States.

The second wave of immigration was quite different from the first. The unification of Italy had brought about tremendous social and economic upheaval which resulted in unprecedented corruption, abuse, and depression. The Italians fleeing from oppression in their native land were an impoverished people, mostly agricultural workers, very often illiterate and ignorant of English. Lacking education or trade experience, they were forced to take the most menial occupations. In New York City they dug the subway tunnels and sewers, and worked in sanitation. Most Italian immigrants of the period were men, ages fourteen to twenty-four, who planned to make a little money and then return to the Old World where they could buy a plot of land or open a store and improve life for themselves and their families.

But the American dream did not come easily. Though mostly of agricultural background, Italians tended to gather in the slum areas of major cities, such as New York, Philadelphia, Boston and Chicago. They faced a host of moral and social problems, as well as the resistance of the peoples who had arrived before, in whose hands rested the wealth and power.

Young Vincent was fortunate to have a craft. For centuries, the Capodanno family had lived by the Gulf of Gaeta and the sea was their way of life. During the first few years after his arrival, he was able to establish himself as a ship caulker on the huge wooden vessels that dotted New York Harbor, the largest and busiest shipyard in the world. He would continue to work on the docks around New York until his death.

The father of the future Medal of Honor winner gave his son not only a seafaring heritage, but one rich in classical myth, military valor, and church history. The town of Gaeta lies on the Tyrrhenian Sea at the southernmost end of the region of Lazio between Rome and Naples. The word "Gaeta" comes from the Latin "Caeta," the name of the wet nurse who tended Aeneas, the mythical hero of Troy and Rome. She was supposedly buried there on Monte d'Orlando where one can also find the classical tomb of the founder of Lyons with its distinctive friezes depicting scenes of battle. A mighty Aragonese castle, impregnable in its day, lords it over the Gulf of Gaeta. The fortress nobly resisted invasions by Goths and Saracens until the Normans finally captured it in 1140. Pope Pius IX took refuge here from 1848–1849 and it was from Gaeta that he published his encyclical *Ubi Primum* on the Immaculate Conception.

Vincent, Sr. worked hard in the years following his arrival, but he managed enough free time to court Rachel Basile, whom he married in 1907 at Sacred Heart, the Basile Family's parish church. He was twenty-two, and she was eighteen. For two generations the Basile family had been in America and all the Basile women, including Rachel's grandmother, had married Italian immigrants at Sacred Heart. At that time, it would have been unthinkable to marry outside one's ethnic group.

While Vincent Capodanno, Jr. would receive from his father a heritage of fortitude and valor, from his mother he would inherit mystery and beauty.

The Basile family originated in Sorrento, Italy, an area of astounding panoramic views and dazzling gardens which lends itself to poetry and art. The 16th century Italian poet Torquato Tasso was born there. Local craftsmen have displayed for centuries their *intarsia* — fine pictures done in inlaid woods, while local laboratories produce perfume and limoncello, the distinctive lemon liquor made from the lemons grown throughout the peninsula. A dramatic tension exists between tranquility and the distant menace of Mt. Vesuvius where towns such as Pompei have sealed in stone the memory of sudden death. For ancient Greeks, the rugged cliffs of Sorrento were the "Temple of the Sirens," maiden-monsters whose beautiful songs lured sailors and their vessels to their doom on the reefs. Homer's Odysseus, determined to hear their singing, plugged up the ears of his men and strapped himself to the mast of his ship as they sailed by. A travel book of 1884 noted the pleasures of a stroll in Sorrento's ravines, "especially in the evening when they have such weirdness and gloominess, that the local people light the lamps in the oratories perched on the rocks, to keep away hobgoblins and foul fiends."

The marriage of Vincent Capodanno from Gaeta to the Sorrentine Rachel Basile brought together the language and liveliness of two Italian sea-faring cultures, preserving a common heritage and keeping the young couple in the secure embrace of the Italian family. For Southern Italians, the family took precedence over every other aspect of life. The individual was socially and interiorly organized around the family — nuclear family first, and then the persons related through marriage and god-parenthood. Within the context of the family an individual derived his status, role, and responsibilities.

In addition, family was inseparably linked to faith. Religion in Italian culture was all pervasive; everything evolved in the context of a religious mystery. There was not a village that lacked its own saints, devotions, and yearly festivals. Italian-American immigrants brought their culture of family and faith to the New World, forming within the structure of the Italian-American parish a tight knit community.

In 1908, Vincent and Rachel Capodanno moved from Brooklyn to Mariners Harbor, Staten Island, the smallest of New York City's five boroughs. It was still a rather rural area — a good place to raise a family. At that time, Staten Island had a population of 85,969 including an increasingly large percentage of Italian-Americans. By the mid-thirties, nearly one third of the white immigrants living on Staten Island had come from Italy, giving the area a strong ethnic identity.

Both Vincent and Rachel worked hard to support their family and put something aside for the future. When he could find it, Vincent jumped at the opportunity to work in the shipyards. He practiced "shaping up," walking from one ship to another to find a day's labor. A second source of income for the Capodannos was their small vegetable store. Selling produce was a common activity of the Italian immigrants of the time, in fact, they virtually had a monoply on the vegetable market in New York. Vincent would rise at 3:00 a.m. to visit the market and purchase the best produce for delivery by horse and wagon to the store; then, he set out for the shipyards, leaving Rachel to look after the day-to-day management of the store.

While the Capodannos concentrated on making ends meet, the world around them was in a boom: the Roaring Twenties. Incomes were up, prices were stable, and chain stores were making things cheaper than ever. Thanks to new techniques of mass production, and cheap immigrant labor, consumer goods were flooding the market. Everyone believed that by shrewd speculation he could be a millionaire and, until then, there was credit. On January 16, 1920, the 18th Amendment banning alcohol became the law of the land and an invitation to bootleggers who made handsome profits when they managed to avoid government agents. Charles Lindbergh made the world a smaller place with his transAtlantic crossing. Babe Ruth and the New York Yankees were the toast of the town. Everyone danced the Charleston, and flagpole sitting was a popular fad.

Throughout this period, the Capodanno clan grew by leaps and bounds. Altogether, Vincent and Rachel had ten children, one of whom died shortly after birth and was not named. Their first, Mary, was born in 1909. She was followed by Pauline, Elinor, Dorothy, James, Gloria, Philip and Albert. Finally, on February 13, 1929, the last child was born and named after his father — Vincent Robert Capodanno, Jr. A neighborhood midwife, another Italian-American, birthed all the boys, including Vincent, in the family home in Elm Park, Staten Island.

The Capodannos were a devout Catholic family. They attended St. Clement's Church, and later, St. Michael's in Mariners Harbor. It was in this last, dedicated to the great commander of the heavenly forces, that Vincent Capodanno, Jr. was baptized on April 28, 1929. By a poetic turn of Providence, the Archdiocese of New York in which Vincent received his faith had been, since 1917, the first seat of the military vicar of the armed forces. It was also the diocese that, in 1911, had welcomed a new religious congregation dedicated to the foreign missions: the Catholic Foreign Mission Society of America — Maryknoll.

In 1929, the year of Vincent, Jr.'s birth, the boom in which his parents had met, married and started a family ended dramatically. On October 29 the stock market crashed, sending the nation and the world into the Great Depression.

The Capodannos, a typical Italian-American family of the time, were buffeted from some of the hardship by the blessings of the hearth, but they could not escape all of it. Into the city came thousands of rural dwellers whose farms collapsed after years of drought. The streets of New York City were lined with apple sellers — people who had once had regular jobs. Employment agencies on 6th Avenue were haunted by jobless New Yorkers; one agency reported an average of 5,000 applicants a day — with only 300 jobs to offer. The flamboyant tunes of the Jazz Age gave way to songs such as "Brother Can You Spare a Dime?"

Vincent and his family watched as Franklin D. Roosevelt's New Deal bore visible results in the New York area. The Public Works Administration, founded in 1933, and the Works Progress Administration, established two years later, were responsible for impressive development projects such as the Municipal Ferryboat, the Triborough Bridge, and the Lincoln Tunnel connecting New York to New Jersey.

Even with the challenges of the Depression, the thirties were a "family time" in many ways. The Capodanno home on Castleton Avenue was always full of activity with nine children, the extended family of aunts, uncles and cousins, and the family sheep dog, Dawny. The family enjoyed being together, playing a game of checkers and listening to the radio. Everyone had their favorite programs: the older folks tuned in to Toscanini's classical symphony, while the younger crowd went for "Your Hit Parade." Everyone enjoyed comics such as Burns and Allen, or Edgar Bergen and Charlie McCarthy. Something good was always cooking in the kitchen, and family meals were times of happy confusion. Being the youngest, and having his father's name, Vincent inevitably became "Junior" and, according to his sister Pauline, the family doted on him.

The warm, loving atmosphere of the Capodan
would impress Vincent's friends in later years when th
panied him home from the seminary or from his ass
The largeness of heart and love of life that characterize the italian-American family were passed on to young Vincent from day
one. As an adult he was noted for showing the same embracing
hospitality to visitors.

Like most Catholics of the time, the family's life unfolded
around the celebration of the Mysteries of the Faith. Every age
had its sacrament. At St. Michael's Church, eight-year-old
Vincent Capodanno made his first Confession and Holy Communion, and received Confirmation — the sacrament that made
him a witness and a soldier for Christ. On Sundays, the family
filled up a pew as they participated in the Holy Sacrifice of the
Mass in the Tridentine Rite. Vincent followed the English trans-
lation of the Latin prayers in his Missal. Symbolism and mystery
surrounded him.

Unlike his brother Philip who was an altar boy and expressed
an interest in the priesthood, Vincent gave no outward sign to his
family during his childhood and adolescence that he ever considered a vocation. Only after high school did he reveal to his friend
William Richter that he had first thought of the priesthood while
in grade school, but had dismissed the idea.

The Capodanno children grew up surrounded with the traditions of a profoundly religious culture. The mysteries of Christ's
life were remembered in the seasons and feasts of the Church
year. Advent, Christmas, Lent and Easter each had their rhythm.
For Italian-Americans the feasts of favorite Italian saints provided the occasion for grand parish festivals. With his sisters and
brothers, Vincent participated in Eucharistic processions, nove-
nas, and charitable bazaars.

The thirties were the beginning of a Golden Age in American
Catholicism. In the early years of the 20th century, the Ku Klux
Klan had worked diligently against blacks, Catholics and Jews
alike and, in 1928, Alfred E. Smith's bid for the presidential
election was marked by bitter anti-Catholic attacks. By the mid-
thirties, however, the climate had changed. As part of a national
religious revival, the Catholic Church stretched her limbs and

showed herself able to penetrate popular culture with her own values. Visible signs of the Church's growth were everywhere. Bishop Dougherty of Philadelphia was responsible for so much construction he earned for himself the title "Bricklayer of God." Movies of the period were highly complimentary of the Church. In films such as "Boys' Town" and "Angels with Dirty Faces" priests were depicted as strong, courageous individuals who possessed solid human virtues while holding onto a firm faith. On the radio, Father Fulton J. Sheen started a career that took him right into the television era, making him one of the most successful broadcasters of all time.

Vincent, Jr. attended Public School 44, a large, four-story, brick building in the borough of Richmond on Staten Island. He was there through eighth grade. An average student, maybe a little better than average, he seemed to struggle only with arithmetic and, even more so, penmanship. Perhaps because of his illegible handwriting, his sister Pauline, who became a nurse, speculated that Vincent had at least one skill necessary to be a doctor.

In appearance, Vincent was a very handsome boy with piercing blue eyes, a tall and slender build — one of the tallest in his class — a soft yet clearly defined face, and a short haircut. He was always neat and well dressed, even at a young age. As the youngest, he received attentive care, especially from his sister Pauline, who would often take him and Albert into New York City and buy them presents. Young Vincent enjoyed swimming and riding his scooter; however, all was not sunshine: just before his tenth birthday, he was struck by a car and seriously injured. The accident resulted in a broken arm and a long period of recuperation during which he fully recovered.

What a time to be a boy! Heroes, both real and imaginary, were clearly defined and the lines were drawn between good guys and bad guys. J. Edgar Hoover and his 600 handpicked G-men squared off against the likes of John Dillinger and Bonnie and Clyde. As brutal as the reality may have been, the images of "true crime" had their romantic side as well and became creative fodder for Hollywood. Actors like Jimmy Cagney and Humphrey Bogart created enduring cultural icons with their pinstriped suits and Tommy Guns.

But more than anything else in the thirties, the heroes of radio captivated the imaginary world of America's youth. Tom Mix assured them, "Lawbreakers always lose, Straight Shooters always win!" Jack Armstrong, "The All American Boy," was a symbol of fair play and patriotism whose exploits took him everywhere in the world. A popular game which appeared as a spin off from the show was the "Chart Game," played on a map of Asian countries including Japan, China, and French Indochina (later, Vietnam). Flash Gordon and Dale Arden were pitted against the Asian-faced Ming the Merciless who was evil incarnate in the thirties as Americans worried more and more about the "Yellow Peril" emerging in Asia.

By the time Vincent Capodanno arrived at the end of his first decade, the world had taken an optimistic stance. The economy was better than it had been before the Crash and advances in technology were promising an easier life for all. But the innocence of the era was about to end. The A-bombs and disintegrator guns that thrilled little boys in Buck Rodgers were ominous presages of the near future.

The relative peace of the Capodanno home ended abruptly on February 13, 1939. While working on a barge on the Hudson River, Vincent Sr. suffered a fatal cerebral hemorrhage. It was his youngest son's tenth birthday. The family waited for their father to come home, especially so that "Junior" could celebrate his big day. Into the night their concern grew. Finally, caring co-workers on the barge notified the family that fifty-three-year-old Vincent, Sr. had been rushed to St. Vincent's hospital in New York City. They arrived at the hospital as quickly as possible, only to be informed that their father had already died. There was no time for good-byes.

Reeling from the sudden and unexpected loss of her husband, Rachel struggled to support the family. With the guidance of their mother's steadfast faith, the children pulled together, unselfishly finding ways to assist her. Further developments in the family followed as the older children, now in their twenties and thirties, started moving out on their own. Soon, world events would bring about even greater changes.

In the same year that the Capodannos lost their father, Germany's tanks rolled into Poland and both France, and England declared war. The nations of Europe fell like dominoes to Hitler's war machine. Feeling safe and secure behind two broad oceans, most Americans hoped they could remain uninvolved in international affairs. Since World War I "isolationism" had been the prevailing political attitude, but the attack on Pearl Harbor on December 7, 1941, marked the end of this philosophy forever.

From the beginning, World War II, unlike other armed conflicts, was represented as a clash between the forces of good — represented by the Allies — and the forces of evil — represented by the Axis powers of Nazi Germany, Fascist Italy and Japan. In 1942 the Bishops of the United States issued a letter declaring the United States "in deadly conflict" against nations which were "united in waging war to bring about a slave world that would deprive man of his divinely conferred dignity, reject human freedom, and permit no religious liberty." Fulton J. Sheen declared the war "a theological one," in which the enemy was "anti-Christ." Archbishop Spellman of New York told troops in Tunisia, "in serving your country in a just cause, you are also serving God."

New heroes emerged for young Vincent Capodanno — and there were plenty to go around. He saw his own big brothers in uniform: two served in the Army and one, James, in the Marine Corps. He waited anxiously with the family for letters from them; he watched the newspapers and listened to the radio for events in far away places that could have serious repercussions for the family. He stood on sidewalks watching parades of crisply marching men about to embark or returning with honor; he heard the patriotic music of military bands. He followed the movements of the great commanders: Eisenhower, Patton and MacArthur. His imagination was fired with stories of Medal of Honor winners like Audie Murphy, one of the most decorated soldiers in American military history. He saw the black wreaths on the doors of homes that had lost a son, brother, husband or father.

Without a doubt, Vincent Capodanno grew up during the most patriotic time in American history. Everyone was making his or her contribution to the war effort. There were Victory Gardens, War Bonds, blood drives, and the work of the Civilian Defense Corps. The popular media also lent a hand with the war effort. Fascists and Japanese were the favorite enemies of funny paper heroes. Even Orphan Annie got into the act encouraging children to join scrap paper drives, while Daddy Warbucks served as a general. Hollywood lost no time churning out movies with patriotic themes, and on the music scene, songs like "This is the Army Mr. Jones" and "Don't Sit under the Apple Tree" described some of the common soldier's concerns.

The war was well covered by the press. Edward R. Murrow broadcast live every evening from London, the wail of air-raid sirens, screaming bombs, and anti-aircraft fire in the background. Each morning the first thing every American did was pick up the paper to follow events on the war front.

In the Pacific, the United States Marine Corps added to an already impressive record with the names of islands claimed one by one at an incredible cost. Twenty-one years later, when Chaplain Vincent Capodanno passed through Okinawa on his way to Vietnam, he would remember the island as the scene of the last and biggest amphibious operation of the Pacific war in which the Marines suffered 19,500 casualties. Ten Marines and three Navy corpsmen received the Congressional Medal of Honor for their actions in Okinawa — eleven posthumously. Vincent would not be alone in his memories of World War II. Twenty years later, the children who had grown up listening to the wartime recollections of their fathers would see in Vietnam an opportunity to realize their own finest hour.

Vincent Capodanno graduated from Public School 44 in January 1943. His graduating class of forty students voted him best looking and best dresser, titles he aptly deserved. He wrote in his school autograph book that his preferred sport was swimming, his favorite song was "The Star Spangled Banner," and his hero was General Douglas MacArthur, who had by then begun his island-hopping campaign in the Pacific. Vincent also noted that he wanted to be a doctor, and he proclaimed his motto to be that of the Cub Scouts: "Do a Good Turn Daily."

Sometimes the comments of youth presage one's future. In the words of young Vincent Capodanno were strands of patriotism, service and compassion. While he never became a physician, he did become a priest, a spiritual healer who was noted by many for his comforting words.

In February 1943, "Vin" entered Curtis Public High School, a large structure, built in the style of a Gothic cathedral. His highest grades were in Latin, yet overall he was not an extraordinary student. During his years at Curtis, he was a class officer, a member of the Biology Honor Society, and a counselor in the CYO. Teenagers were a distinct social entity in the forties. They gathered together at soda shops or wherever a jukebox could be found — sloppy trousers, loafers and dangling shirttails the fashion of the day. Vincent's social life was somewhat limited because of his after-school job in a local drug store.

In the early morning before attending school, he would regularly go to Mass at his home parish, Our Lady of Good Counsel Church in Tompkinsville, New York. To keep the pre-Communion fast, he would carry his breakfast — usually a hard-boiled egg — in his pocket.

The war ended in summer of 1945, midway through Vincent's high school career. The simple life of America in the thirties had passed through the bloody conflict of the forties into a world of ambiguity and suspicion, a situation which would worsen in the next decade as Vincent devoted himself to his seminary studies. In particular, two menaces faced the world: the possibility of complete annihilation by nuclear bombs, and the threat of communism as it swallowed up what was left of the European people after the war. The Marshall Plan was heralded as a bulwark against communism, and new heroes emerged amongst those resisting its advance. But for the most part, people were enjoying the relief and hope of an era marked by revived economic opportunity and a victory over the specter of world evil.

After completing high school in February 1947, Vincent worked as a popular and trusted underwriting clerk at the Pearl Insurance Company on Maiden Lane near the Wall Street district. He also sought to continue the education his parents valued so highly, attending night classes in the School of Education at Fordham University in downtown Manhattan. Clerk by day and student by night, Vincent was able to contribute to the support of the family.

During this year, Vincent met William Richter, who had also gone to Curtis High School, although they had not known each other at the time. The two became life-long friends. Every morning at 8:00 a.m., they went together to Mass at Our Lady of Victory Church and shared breakfast afterwards. At the end of the working day, before classes, they would meet again at Church for benediction, and frequently for Confession. Ordinarily, they would travel home together on the half-hour Staten Island ferry ride, passing beneath the outstretched arm and welcoming beacon of the Statue of Liberty.

In the spring of 1949, at a parish near the Williamsburg Bridge in Manhattan, the two friends made a retreat together. During the retreat, Vincent confided to William his great desire to become a priest, a desire he had kept silent for years and often dismissed. William described his friend as an unassuming, down to earth young man whose devout, Catholic life was evident. He had a humble, deep relationship with Christ. By the time of their retreat, Vincent felt himself drawn to a new level, one he felt ready for — the priesthood.

One night, on the ferry to Staten Island, Vincent turned to William and said in his characteristically quiet tone, "Bill, I think you have a vocation, too." William's first impulse was to dismiss his friend's odd remark as simply crazy. Years later however, speaking as an ordained Catholic priest, William Richter acknowledged that Capodanno's suggestion was the pivotal point: "He did plant the idea and, after some discernment . . . I decided to enter the Maryknoll seminary."

Richter also remembered Vincent Capodanno's deep affection and solicitous concern for his mother. He worked hard to support her and felt personally responsible for her. Out of his great love for his mother, aware that his leaving would cause her pain, Vincent delayed his entry into the seminary a full year.

The call to the priesthood can be as different as the men who are called. Usually, it comes as a kind of interior clamor that cannot be silenced. Very commonly, the initial reaction is to deny the possibility that God is actually the source of the idea. A young man who suspects he has the call to priestly service must enter a time of prayerful reflection known as discernment. And when he is finally ready to answer the call, there are other questions: What kind of priest does God want me to be? Should I become a diocesan priest, or a religious? If religious, what order should I join?

Vincent and William both entered into this period of discernment. Richter said of his friend, "He is an unforgettable example to me of someone who followed the call to serve, wherever it might eventually lead him, a call that refused to go away."

In Vincent's case, the choice of where to live out his priesthood was not too difficult — in fact, it had been in his mind for some time. There was hardly a Catholic in the United States who did not know the name of The Catholic Foreign Mission Society of America, or more popularly, Maryknoll, and most read the Society's inspiring and adventurous publication *The Field Afar*. This popular monthly magazine astounded its audience with stories of daring priests at work for the Lord in previously unimaginable lands such as China, Japan, Africa, Manchuria and the Philippines. Before *National Geographic* was a staple of the American home, here were gripping accounts interspersed with bright and colorful pictures of strange people and exotic lands. Its loyal readership provided the Society not only with a steady source of donations, but also with a constant flow of applicants who wanted to join Maryknoll. As Vincent himself wrote on his application in response to the question, "Why do you want to become a Maryknoll missioner?":

> I first heard of the Maryknoll through *Field Afar*. I became acquainted with the kind of work they do and the lives they lead. I admired them for it but never thought too much about it. When I decided to go into the foreign mission field I remembered all I had read about the Maryknolls [sic][1] and decided that that was what I wanted to do.

Given his solid Catholic upbringing, and the high ideals inspired in him by his times, it is not surprising that Vincent Capodanno would feel the attraction in this exciting and challenging missionary career that seemed to imitate the sacrificial life of Christ more completely than any other service within the Church. It meant being on the cutting edge of the Gospel imperative: to bring the message of salvation to all nations. Missionary life was an invitation to explore the uncharted waters of the world, as well as one's own faith in Christ.

His application was sent to Maryknoll for review along with letters of recommendations from his pastor, Father James H. Griffin of Our Lady of Good Counsel Parish; Mr. John M. Avent, his high school principal; and Father John J. Hooper, a Jesuit and Assistant Dean at Fordham University, who noted that, while he did not know Vincent that well, he did know him "to be a quiet, refined young man, who averages B's and has been interested in Maryknoll for some time."

All seemed in good order for Vincent to enter the Society's seminary except for one minor difficulty: Mrs. Capodanno did not want Vincent to leave and enroll in such a seemingly dangerous vocation — one that would take him far from home. Father Walter Maxey visited Vincent's Staten Island home to calm Mrs. Capodanno's fears. Father Maxey wrote to Father Smith, the Vocation Director for Maryknoll: "[The] mother feels that he is being a bit selfish to leave her. [However,] the mother won't stand in his way. Not a lack of faith, just expecting the worse [sic]."

Vincent was formally accepted to The Catholic Foreign Mission Society of America on May 17, 1949. Before leaving home for the seminary, Vincent had only one special request of his family: when the family would come to visit him at school he asked that they not embarrass him by calling him "Junior."

Faith and patriotism were now joined to evangelical zeal in the twenty-year-old Capodanno and his desire for self-donation took the form of a priestly life of service in fields afar. In Maryknoll, Vincent found the ministry that responded to his deepest stirrings; in fact, the very roots of Vincent's future actions and thoughts are reflected in the history, conviction, and spirituality of Maryknoll. The man Vincent would become over the next nine years of formation and subsequent missionary work was greatly shaped by the vision and direction of this dedicated mission society.

In his own words, written on his application to Maryknoll, in answer to the question: "What is your idea of the life and work of a foreign missioner?" he says:

It will mean hard physical labor with and for a group of people I may never have even heard of before. I'll be separated from my family and friends, and all the things I'm now accustomed to, for indefinite lengths of time, during which all my efforts will be devoted to the people I'm serving. Their lives, both troubles and joys will be my life. Any personal sacrifice I may have to make will be compensated for by the fact that I am serving God.

One can see clearly that there was nothing weak or timid about Vincent Capodanno's call to the priesthood. He knew the work of a missionary meant "hard physical labor" and that he would ultimately be separated from those he knew and loved in order to serve distant and unfamiliar peoples. He understood that it was a call to the ultimate sacrifice — giving one's life for others. In Vincent's case, that call had to be answered in the most radical way, on a spiritual battlefield in foreign lands.

RADIATING CHRIST

They will be chosen men, it is true; God will care-fully select the official ministers of the Word. He will fit them by a special training for their apostolic work; they will be qualified men. The Church will have a body of teachers whose official function will be to dis-tribute the truth; they are the priests.

Raoul Plus, S.J.,
Radiating Christ: An Appeal to Militant Catholics

To enter the Maryknoll headquarters in Ossining, New York, the visitor passes through Chinese fretted front doors and into a rotunda. In the center of the floor rests a bronze circle on the top half of which is written "Pax Intrantibus" or "Peace to those who enter." Appropriate words for a missionary seminary, from which priests would go forth announcing to all on behalf of God, "Peace be with you!" The peace they would offer, however, would not be that which the world can give; it was purchased by Christ on his Cross and given to the apostles as the first gift of his Resurrection. From the first Christian martyr onward, the Church's history would be rich in men and women who knew the true meaning of peace and were willing to witness to it with their lives.

The history of Maryknoll abounds with such heroes: Father Jerry Donovan, Father Sandy Cairns, Father William Cummings, Bishop Patrick J. Byrne, Bishop Francis Xavier Ford, and so many others. The founding members of Maryknoll responded to-tally to Christ's challenge of peace. They were courageous men whose stories have the power to inspire us even now.

Maryknoll began in the hearts of two priests who were truly ahead of their time. At the turn of the century, the United States was still officially a missionary country and consequently under the Congregation for the Propagation of the Faith in Rome. Not until 1908 did the Vatican finally pronounce the United States a non-missionary area. During this same year, Father Thomas Frederick Price, the first priest ordained in North Carolina, began to envision a seminary to instruct men for the foreign missions. Up north, Father James Walsh also had his mind on the missions. The same desire grew simultaneously in the hearts of these men, even though they were separated by distance.

Thomas Frederick Price was born in Wilmington, North Carolina on August 19, 1860, the eighth child of Alfred and Clarissa Bond Price. His parents were converts to Roman Catholicism and he was raised as a devout Catholic in the midst of a Southern culture that was at best apathetic to the Church and at worst hostile. He grew up in the parish of St. Thomas and attended Mass regularly, serving as an altar boy to Father James Gibbons who, in addition to being a life-long friend, would later become a cardinal and a great support in the formation of Maryknoll.

On his way to the seminary, Price nearly lost his life when a storm caused his ship to founder. He would always owe his salvation to the miraculous intervention of the Blessed Mother, and throughout his life would enjoy a profoundly intimate relationship with her. A few months later, he made the trip again — this time on land. He graduated in 1881 from St. Charles College and then went on to St. Mary's Seminary close by, receiving ordination on June 20, 1886.

Price returned to his home state with one intention in mind: to convert everyone. The odds were against him; but Price's relentless efforts, unbounded optimism, and good humor won over the suspicious North Carolinians. In a state that had about 800 Catholics, he conceived the plan to publish a Catholic magazine which would give reasons for the Catholic faith. Already in *The Truth* it is apparent that Price was imbued with the spirit of the missions. In 1909, he wrote the following prophetic declaration and challenge in *The Truth*:

At the present time, the Church in the United States is sending out almost no missioners to foreign countries. In a few years this is likely to be changed. We look for the Roman Catholics of the United States to become the greatest mission force in the world, and therein lies the salvation of the Church in the United States.

There is no doubt that the roots of Maryknoll are planted in the personal holiness of this extraordinary man. Quiet and unassuming, he asked that his name and picture never appear in *The Field Afar*. Price's interiority made him rather unconcerned for exterior realities. He was mindless of his appearance, schedules, and administrative details. It made little difference to him what he ate and he had no conception of money. His quarters were a disorganized heap of books and papers. Yet, his warmth and good humor always shone out over his shortcomings.

In total contrast to Father Price, Father James Anthony Walsh was a meticulous, carefully refined gentleman and a born administrator with a passion for detail. It is said that while speaking to seminarians on the Resurrection, he was quick to point out that when the Apostle John arrived at the empty tomb he discovered the linens which had covered the body of the Lord neatly wrapped, and the napkin — which had been placed about Christ's head — folded in a separate place. "Please note," he told his students, "that the napkin was *folded* and in its proper place."

Father Walsh was born on February 24, 1867, the son of Irish immigrants James Walsh and Hanna Shea. He grew up in the Boston area where he attended first the public schools and then Boston College High School. Early on, his gifts for debating and writing were apparent. After high school he began at Boston College but transferred to Harvard for a short while. Finally, he completed his studies at St. John's Seminary in Brighton, Massachusetts and was ordained on May 20, 1892.

Father Walsh was inspired toward the mission field by his rector at St. Johns, Abbé Hogan, a French priest of the Sulpician order who was filled with stories of the Paris Foreign Mission Society's work in Indochina. After his ordination in 1892, Father Walsh was assigned to Saint Patrick's parish in Roxbury, Massachusetts. Not until 1902, when he was asked to head the Boston branch of the Society for the Propagation of the Faith, was he able to continue his interest in the foreign missions. During his tenure with the Society, Father Walsh began the publication of *The Field Afar* in order to generate interest in supporting foreign missionaries in their work. He also traveled to Europe and met the various mission societies of the time.

Fathers Price and Walsh, both of them at a turning point in their lives, met in Montreal at the Eucharistic Congress of 1910. They marveled and rejoiced at the complementary nature of their ideas about foreign mission work. They realized that this was the beginning of a shared goal — the foundation of an American missionary seminary.

Soon after the Congress, Father Walsh approached William Cardinal O'Connell, the Archbishop of Boston and his former classmate, and James Cardinal Gibbons of the Archdiocese of Baltimore, with the idea of founding an American missionary society. Both men received the proposal favorably. The next step was to gain the approval of the rest of the American hierarchy. At their Washington, D.C., meeting in April 1911, the bishops unanimously approved the plan.

The only remaining hurdle was Hieronimus Marie Cardinal Gotti, the Vatican's Prefect for the Sacred Congregation of Propaganda. Speaking for Pope Pius X, he would be the one to grant final approval.

Fathers Price and Walsh arrived in Rome on June 18, 1911. Knowing the maternal caution of the Church, and the length of time that it usually took for hierarchical Rome to act on something, they believed their chances for success were limited and that the approval process could take months or even years. But just eleven days after their arrival, on the feast of Saints Peter and Paul, the two priests had their last meeting with Cardinal Gotti who informed them that the Holy Father was delighted to learn of such a cause and ready to fully approve the plan. On June 29, 1911, the Catholic Foreign Mission Society of America was born.

Formal establishment now accomplished, the work of putting together a functioning society began. The first office was located temporarily in the village of Hawthorne, New York, about twenty-nine miles north of New York City. In 1912, the Society moved to its present location in Ossining, New York. Ninety-three acres, three houses, and an old barn became the seminary property on the ridge of Sunset Hill overlooking the picturesque Hudson River. Father Walsh was to nickname the hill "Mary's Knoll," and the name has been used ever since to identify the Society.

Now, the Society needed seminarians. Father Walsh announced the formation of Maryknoll in *The Field Afar* and issued an invitation for young men to join the Society. The notice read:

> Youths or young men who feel a strong desire to toil for the souls of heathen people and who are willing to go afar with no hope of earthly recompense and with no guarantee of a return to their native land are encouraged to write, making their letter personal, to the Editor of *Field Afar*.

Six seminarians began studies that fall of 1912. The first student accepted was Francis Ford from the Cathedral College in New York City. The second was a young man from Mount Saint Mary College in Emmitsburg, Maryland, James Edward Walsh, whose name would be continually confused with the Society's Superior.

Six years later, the first group of Maryknoll missionaries left to take up work at a mission in China. They included Fathers Price, Ford, James Edward Walsh, and Bernard F. Meyer of Iowa. Father Price's life-long passion for mission work culminated in this assignment, but it was to be his Gethsemane. Because of his age, Price had great difficulty learning the Chinese language; he did not adjust well to the climate and his health, already precarious, declined rapidly. He died in Hong Kong, September 12, 1919, almost a year to the day after he had first arrived.

Father Price's death was a great personal loss to Father Walsh. One of the touching aspects of the Maryknoll story is the mutual respect and friendship between these two men, so different in personality, but of one heart in their desire to spread the Gospel. Made a bishop in 1933, Walsh would continue to serve until his death at Maryknoll on April 14, 1936.

Vincent Capodanno never met the founders of Maryknoll, but curiously, his temperament seemed to be a blend of both. He had the gentlemanly deportment and affection for order of Father

Walsh, and the inner calm and desire for sacrifice of Father Price. He must have taken great consolation in the memory of Father Price's struggle with Chinese when he himself would face the challenges of the Hakka dialect in Taiwan.

When Vincent Capodanno entered Maryknoll in 1949, the Society had been in existence for only thirty-eight years, but it had become one of the fastest growing religious communities for men in the history of the Church in the United States. Within a short span of time, Maryknollers were making a name for themselves by their heroic witness to their faith, inspiring other young men to follow.

The letter from Father James F. Smith, the Vocation Director of Maryknoll, which welcomed Vincent to the Society, also informed him that he was to begin his studies sooner than expected. To make up credits he lacked in Latin, he was required to enter a Maryknoll summer school. Knowing the difficulty that his mother had with his entering the missionary life, Father Smith apologized to Vincent for cutting short his last full summer vacation at home.

The formation of a missionary like Vincent, who arrived shortly after high school, took altogether nine years. It was rigorous and thorough, emphasizing both the theory and practice. It might better be called an apprenticeship. There were three stages: first, four years of college seminary leading to a Bachelor's Degree in Philosophy; novitiate, which consisted of one year of intense personal prayer and reflection, as well as studies on the nature and history of the Maryknoll mission; and finally, major seminary, three years of study culminating in a graduate degree in Theology. In addition to this, the missionary would have one year of language study in the territory to which he was assigned before beginning his actual duties there.

On June 25, 1949, Vincent Capodanno began the process when he arrived at his summer school, the Maryknoll Junior Seminary in Clarks Summit, Pennsylvania. This high school preparatory seminary, with a capacity for 160 students, opened in 1913 in the hardscrabble anthracite coal region near the city of Scranton. The Junior Seminary existed for the instruction and formation of high-school aged boys who expressed an interest in the priesthood and showed promise as a missionary.

The seminary was affectionately called "The Vénard," after Blessed Theophane Vénard (1829–1861), a young French missionary who was martyred in Tonkin — a part of the present country of Vietnam. Blessed Vénard was Bishop Walsh's favorite example of a true missionary. He had written a book on Vénard and included him in his *Thoughts from Modern Martyrs*. He also wrote the short article on Vénard in the Catholic Encyclopedia of 1912.

Blessed Venard's spirit and memory was an integral part of Maryknoll formation and would have been an inspiration to Vincent Capodanno and his classmates. There was something striking about the young Frenchman's gallantry in facing his own death. Shortly after his arrival in Tonkin a new royal edict was issued against Christians. Bishops and priests were forced to seek refuge in the wilderness. Father Vénard, whose health was delicate to begin with, suffered almost constantly from the difficult living conditions, but he would sneak out at night to continue exercising his ministry. Finally, betrayed and captured, he refused to apostatize and was condemned to be beheaded. The sentence was delayed. During his long wait on death row he lived in a cage from which he wrote to his family beautiful and consoling letters, joyfully anticipating his heavenly reward. On the way to martyrdom, he chanted psalms and hymns. The executioner asked Vénard what he would give him to be killed quickly, but the young priest, seeing in his death an act of prayer and praise, responded, "The longer it lasts, the better!"

While Latin was Vincent's best subject in high school, it was definitely a difficult course for him at the summer school in Clarks Summit. He received a final grade of seventy-seven. The weeks must have gone by slowly as he struggled to adjust to seminary life, a demanding Latin teacher and — at a hundred miles from home — his first extended separation from his family. On August 3, Vincent finished his session and was able to return to Staten Island. The Vénard had given him a taste of what to anticipate in the fall, as well as during the next nine years of study and formation required before ordination. He enjoyed the remainder of his summer while continuing to work part-time for the Pearl Insurance Company.

While at home in August, Vincent received another letter from Father Kiernan who had now been named Rector and Superior General of Maryknoll College in Glen Ellyn, Illinois — Vincent's next stop. Father wrote that the seminary was still under construction and would not be ready to receive seminarians until the beginning of October. His departure delayed, the twenty-year-old reclaimed the month with his family he had forfeited when he went to summer school.

Vincent's close friend and fellow Maryknoll candidate, William Richter, was also preparing to enter his first year of study for Maryknoll. They had hoped to be in the same school, but unlike Capodanno, who knew a little Latin, Richter knew none. He was sent to Brookline, Massachusetts, for an extensive one-year Latin program.

In the fall of 1949, Vincent Capodanno arrived at the newly renovated Maryknoll College in Glenn Ellyn, Illinois. While the property, located nearly an hour from Chicago, was bought in 1944, most of the colonial-style buildings were erected after the war. The college was built to house 300 seminarians, and during Vincent's time there the enrollment was always at full capacity.

Vincent's first two years of college were devoted to basic liberal arts subjects: European History, Chemistry, English Literature and, in every semester, Latin. He was an average student, usually ranking in the middle of his eighty-five-member class. His highest grade by far was in "The Life of Christ: The Mass," for which he received a ninety-seven in one semester and ninety-two in the other.

For his sophomore year, Vincent was transferred to Maryknoll Junior College in Lakewood, New Jersey. He continued his studies there, making friends among the sixty-six seminarians in his class, until the fall of 1951 when he returned to Glenn Ellyn for his junior year. Joining him at the college finally was his good friend William Richter. Together they started a two-year study of philosophy. All seminarians took such classes as Ancient and Medieval Philosophy, Metaphysics and Logic to lay a solid foundation on which they could build during graduate theology studies.

The faculty was interested not only in the academic progress of the seminarians, but also in their spiritual growth. The seminarians participated in daily Mass, periods of prayer, and long sessions of silence. The challenge was compounded by Maryknoll's policy of accepting candidates from all walks of life — including doctors, lawyers, soldiers and young men like Vincent. Each individual candidate had to be molded into a deeply motivated priest for the service of souls in all lands. A 1958 Maryknoll book says, "[The] final aim is to develop a priest who will possess sympathy for his people, a readiness to forget himself in helping them, courage in the face of obstacles, humility in success and confidence in spite of apparent failure."

In a few years, these college students would be advocates for Christ in countries that might or might not accept the Gospel message. The seminary was training them for all possibilities and inevitable adversities, producing leaders who could function on their own even in arduous situations. And so, not surprisingly, seminary life at Maryknoll had something of the atmosphere of a military academy: discipline was strict; expectations for performance were high. Bishop James E. Walsh, one of Maryknoll's first missionaries, noted: "The seminary is not simply a house of prayer and study; it is also a laboratory where soul-strengthening and mind-sharpening activities are utilized for the formation of the missionary character."

An outstanding witness to this missionary character, as well as an inspiration and a model to Vincent Capodanno and his classmates, was Bishop Francis Xavier Ford, member of the first Maryknoll group sent to China in 1918. Consecrated Bishop of Kaying in 1935, Ford chose as his Episcopal motto "To suffer with," prophetic words for this shepherd who would not abandon his people during persecution. In December 1950, the Communists in Canton, China imprisoned Ford and his private secretary, Maryknoll Sister Joan Marie. They both endured terrible tortures, beatings, and humiliating marches through the Canton streets. On his way to confinement Bishop Ford said to Sister Joan Marie, "We're going to prison in honor of Christ. It's no disgrace." The whole Maryknoll family, including Vincent

Capodanno and his classmates, awaited news of their brother and sister in chains. Though Sister Joan Marie would survive, the continuous interrogations and starvation diet were too much for Bishop Ford and he finally died in 1952.

The seminarians had another striking example of fidelity to the missionary character in Bishop Patrick J. Byrne. Byrne had been amongst the founding students at Maryknoll, coming to them as an already ordained priest — the first to do so. After ten years of administrative work and teaching, in which he selflessly gave up his dreams of the missions to build up the Society, he was assigned to Korea in 1923. Bishop Byrne spent many years in the Orient, filling different posts — most notably in Japan; finally, he returned to the sight of his first assignment in Korea. In 1950, Communists in that country crossed the 38th parallel, initiating a terrible conflict with the United States and a vigorous persecution of Christians. Bishop Byrne, with other priests and Chinese Christians, was forced to march in the winter snow along the Yalu River. Many died of exposure or were shot on the way. The Bishop himself succumbed to pneumonia in November 1950 after being forced to exercise in freezing weather. His last words were addressed to his fellow priests: "I consider it the greatest privilege of my life to have suffered together with you for Christ."

These two seminal events in Maryknoll history brought home to each seminarian the true meaning of discipleship, even as the political context in which they occurred reflected a changing order on the world stage into which the Maryknollers ventured. Vincent Capodanno and his classmates must have privately questioned themselves: "Will I be able to suffer with and for the people of foreign lands? Will I give the ultimate witness to the Gospel by martyrdom?" For Capodanno, the conflict in Vietnam would be an invitation "to suffer with."

Not everyone, however, is called to shed his blood for the Gospel. For most, the sacrifice of a faithful life is what is asked. Bishop James Walsh's motto, "Seek First the Kingdom of God," is also the motto of Maryknoll because a missionary's ultimate goal is not found here in this passing world but with God in heaven. "The only important thing to think of is the Kingdom of

God, in the world and in our heart," said Bishop Walsh. He further explained his motto during one of his Sunday conferences:

> Very few of us will actually shed blood for Christ, but there is none of us who will not have the opportunity to thin out his blood for Christ . . . the spiritual suffering and moral trials we may have to endure are by far the most difficult.

According to his friends, Vincent enjoyed these years of preparation. Fellow student Don Sheehan remembered Vincent Capodanno as a regular guy — not very athletic, neat and meticulous in manner and dress as in high school, and one who enjoyed smoking during the few periods in the day when it was allowed. He also had the reputation of being quite an actor. One semester he appeared in the play *Savonarola*, a one-man show derived from speeches of the ill-fated 15th century Dominican.

While exclusive friendships were discouraged in the seminary for the sake of building up the whole community, Capodanno did have a few close classmates. John Rich from nearby Chicago would often take Capodanno — known as "Vinnie" or "Vince" in the seminary — to his home over the short breaks and free weekends. Later, when the two were studying theology in Ossining, Vincent reciprocated by taking Rich either to his mother's home on Staten Island, or over to his sister Pauline's house in Kearny, New Jersey, where they swam in a neighbor's pool. Both John Rich and William Richter remembered that it was always enjoyable to visit the Capodannos and sit down to a delicious Italian meal. Richter later recalled the "many Sunday afternoons I spent at Vince's home, at the dining room table there with his mother, his brothers, and his sisters." The friendships forged among these Maryknollers would last a lifetime and carry them through the times of discernment and doubt.

During their summer breaks from school, the seminarians were allowed to spend part of their time at home working at summer jobs. Vincent would return to the Pearl Insurance Company; they were always willing to rehire him because he was dependable.

He also got together over vacations with his fellow Maryknollers, including William Richter, who lived in the New

York City area. As before their entry into Maryknoll, Vincent and William would often attend daily Mass together at the parish church of Our Lady of Good Counsel. On Friday evenings they made it a practice to attend devotions at Our Lady of Mount Carmel Church, an Italian parish near Vincent's home.

The college days passed quickly for John Rich, William Richter, Vincent Capodanno and all their classmates. In the spring of 1953, Vincent received his Bachelor of Arts degree with a major in philosophy. He started college with eighty-four classmates, but only thirty-eight — less than half the original enrollment — graduated. The purpose of a seminary is not only to provide a place of education and formation, but also to offer a haven for discernment, for prayerfully thinking through a young man's initial commitment. Many would face the disappointing realization that they were not called to the priesthood or that they were not cut out for the demanding life of a missionary. Vincent Capodanno's vocation held firm. He was ready to begin his novitiate in Bedford, Massachusetts.

In religious life, the novitiate is a one-year period in which candidates take time out of their academic studies to concentrate on their spiritual life through quiet discernment and the study of the history and constitution of the religious congregation to which they belong. A seminarian by this point has had a chance to experience what priestly life means. He must now listen again to his heart — even if it struggles with some elements of the life he knows he will be living. He must discern if this is the vocation God has given him and, in prayer, find the source of divine grace that will make fidelity to that call possible.

One of the tasks assigned to seminarians during their novitiate year was the making of appeals for Maryknoll. An appeal consisted of visiting a parish and sharing with the parishioners the work of Maryknoll, inviting them to participate by an offering of prayer or financial support. One Sunday in 1953, seminarians Vincent Capodanno and William Richter were sent to make such an appeal to Sacred Heart parish in Brooklyn, the same parish where Vincent's parents had been married. They enjoyed the experience, especially the fact that everyone prematurely mistook them for priests and called them "Father."

August 1954 marked the end of the novitiate. Again, some seminarians during this time of spiritual reflection faced the difficult discovery that they were not called to this demanding way of priestly life. It must have been a hard fact for these young men to accept. Hard, too, must have been the good-byes. They had come a long way together. Particularly difficult for Vincent Capodanno was saying farewell to his oldest and closest friend in the seminary: William Richter. Richter realized he must be among those who left Maryknoll, though he would continue towards ordination as a diocesan priest in Toledo, Ohio. Thirty-six years later, Father Richter noted, "With great love and great spiritual example, I feel that I owe my vocation to the priesthood to him [Vincent Capodanno]."

In August of 1953, his college studies and novitiate over, Vincent took the first of three oaths stating his free desire to continue studying for the Society. In the fall, he began his first year of theology at Maryknoll's major seminary in Ossining, New York.

The seminary building in Ossining — a small town better known for its prison, Sing Sing — also serves as the headquarters for the Society. This imposing edifice with its many symbolic furnishings is as much a statement about being a missionary as any book or spiritual practice. The construction of it began in 1920 and continued until 1956. The stone façade is a true marriage between oriental and Roman architecture, the oriental motif constantly reminding the seminarians that their main goal did not lie here in America, but in distant lands.

The greeting above the entrance, "Go And Teach All Nations," is the Gospel imperative of Christ and the main mission of Maryknoll. Even the name of the main chapel, "Queen of Apostles," reminded the soon-to-be missionaries of the great duty ahead. The crypt, located near the founders' tomb, is devoted to twenty-four missionaries from the annals of Church history. Close to the great altar of the main chapel is the chapel dedicated to "Mary, Queen of Martyrs" with stained glass windows displaying the Seven Sorrows of Mary. The Crypt of the Apostles shows in symbols the martyrdom suffered by eleven of the twelve Apostles. St. John was spared martyrdom, but lived to old age nurturing the infant Christian community.

The seminarians had much to reflect upon in the Martyrs' Shrine containing the relics of fifty-one saints and martyrs. A visit to the cemetery dramatized even more the cost of a missionary's commitment. One of the graves is that of Father Gerard Donovan, the first of many Maryknollers killed proclaiming the word of God. He died by strangulation in October 1937 near his Hopie Mission in China, his body left to the beasts of the forest before it was finally found by his friends and brought home.

Life in Ossining was demanding; the daily schedule allowed little free time. Each seminarian rose at 5:30 a.m. for morning prayers, meditation and Mass. He donned a black cassock, which would be worn all day. Breakfast followed, during which students listened to diaries written by Maryknollers in the field. They learned how the Society was built and, at the same time, received a realistic picture of missionary life. After the meal, each seminarian was expected to perform some job or cleaning duty. The purpose of this work was to expose them to a wide variety of jobs that would be useful to missionaries in the field, such as farming, carpentry, and maintenance.

Classes filled the rest of the morning. The studies of major seminary are specifically directed to a man's education as priest, since he is called to dispense the mysteries of Christ. As St. Peter exhorts, "Always be ready . . . to account for the hope that is in you." (1 Peter 3:15) Classes included Sacred Scripture, Moral Theology, Canon Law (the rules of governance for the Catholic Church), Liturgy and Homiletics (preaching).

At noon, a period of prayer in chapel was followed by lunch, and then another hour of manual labor. After the work was finished, seminarians were allowed an hour of recreation; usually they played sports such as basketball and handball. The rest of the afternoon was filled with more classes and study periods. The Rosary was said at 5:30 p.m., followed by a conference from the spiritual director. After supper, there was a half-hour recreation period and then another study hall. The day closed with night prayer at 9:00 p.m., followed by lights out.

During this period in their education, the seminarians were

also sent on various pastoral assignments over the summer. Vincent taught catechism, visited prisoners and received basic medical training at a hospital.

Because of the year-round study and training required, time at home was limited to one month every summer. Whenever possible, Vincent's attentive mother came to Ossining to visit him. Mrs. Capodanno was not in the best of health, so her daughter Pauline Costa and Pauline's husband, George, who was a doctor, would care for her and bring her to the seminary.

The Capodanno family was a constant in Vincent's life. He could always count on them. During his time as a seminarian, he received generous support, both financially and morally, from his mother and from the Costas. This help continued long after he was ordained. He was forever grateful and showed his appreciation by his frequent letters and prayers as a typical note to his sister indicates: "Thanks for your Christmas present. I intend to use part of it [the money] to pay for my breviaries. Come next June when I begin to say the Divine Office every day you can count on being prayed for in my Office."

When Vincent did get home, he also took every opportunity to see his friend William Richter. Richter noted that during one of the summer breaks they went to see the French film "Monsieur Vincent," the life of Saint Vincent de Paul (1567–1622). It had a profound impact on both of them, but especially on Capodanno, who was named after this bishop and Church writer who devoted his life to the alleviation of human suffering and misery.

In the final years of his academic preparation, Vincent also advanced through the minor orders in the Church. Prior to the reforms of Vatican Council II, men en route to the priesthood passed through specific orders, or functions, which symbolized their increasing proximity to the sacrament of ordination. In our time, lay people regularly fill these duties. Yet, there was a wonderful pedagogical usefulness in the minor orders. Vincent would have understood that each order brought him closer to being a priest, and the exercise of his responsibilities at each level would have made him more comfortable with his position as a minister of the sacred mysteries.

The first stage was that of Porter, or doorkeeper, whose duties were to ring the bell, open the church and sacristy, and open the book for the preacher. The order of Lector followed, in which the candidate received a special blessing for the reading of scripture in the Liturgy. The position of Exorcist was closely associated with the baptismal rite. The last minor order, that of Acolyte, brought the seminarian into close contact with the altar. His chief duties were to light the candles and carry them in procession, prepare wine and water for the sacrifice of the Mass, and assist the priests at the Mass and other public services of the Church. Nowadays, altar servers fill the role of Acolyte.

Following completion of the minor orders, Vincent then proceeded to the first of the three major orders, that of Sub-deacon. He would carry the chalice filled with wine to the altar, prepare the necessities for the celebration of the Eucharist, and read the Epistles before the people. Then, as now, actual participation in Holy Orders began with ordination to the Diaconate. On June 6, 1957, Vincent Capodanno was ordained a deacon and made his lifelong commitment to remain with Maryknoll. He had only one year left before he would be ordained a priest and receive his first mission assignment.

This last year of seminary was difficult for Vincent because of his mother's failing physical condition after a fall had broken her hip. The family was financially strapped from the expenses of her long hospitalization. Vincent took the responsibility and asked for and received an interest-free, one-year loan of $1,000 from Maryknoll to help pay for part of the medical expenses. Maryknoll also gave him leave time so he could be with his mother. Pauline remembered that Vincent was a devoted and attentive son who spent hour after hour with his mother, giving her comfort and encouragement.

Ordination day was truly an end and a beginning: the end of nine years of study, prayer and discernment; the beginning of a new way of life. No longer could Vincent Capodanno follow the comfortable daily routines of seminary life; he now had to face the unknown challenges of his missionary assignment. His studies would now be taken from theory to practice, from the classroom to the missionary field.

On Saturday, June 14, 1958, the whole Capodanno clan gathered for the three hour Ordination ceremony at the main Maryknoll chapel, "Mary, Queen of Apostles." Mrs. Capodanno had to attend in a wheelchair because of her weak hip. The day was warm and the chapel packed, as forty-eight men received ordination from Francis Cardinal Spellman, the Archbishop of New York.

The symbols of the Ordination Rite expressed the meaning of priesthood and the history of the Church. The candidates presented themselves in clerical dress, carrying their priestly vestments over one arm, and holding lighted candles. Each was summoned by name, answering in Latin, "Adsum" (Here I Am!). The Bishop inquired of all present if these men were worthy to be admitted to the priesthood.

The Ordination ceremony then moved into its most moving symbolism. The *ordinandi*, those to be ordained, laid themselves prostrate on the floor, manifesting their submission to Christ the high priest, and their readiness to imitate his self-emptying in their own lives. As they lay there, faces to the ground, they listened to the choir singing the Litany of the Saints, recalling one after another the men and women who down through the centuries had given witness to the Gospel.

The climatic moment arrived. Vincent rose, came forward and knelt before the Bishop, who placed his hands on his head and prayed silently. This gesture was then imitated by all priests present. The Bishop then took Father Vincent's stole and crossed it over his breast; he placed the chasuble over the new priest's head saying, "Take thou the priestly vestment whereby charity is signified; for God is well able to give thee an increase of charity and its perfect works." A few moments later, Father Vincent again approached the Bishop, who anointed his open hands, tracing a cross upon them with the Holy Oils, and binding them together with a white cloth. "Be pleased, O Lord, to consecrate and hallow these hands ... that whatsoever they bless may be blessed, and whatsoever they consecrate may be consecrated and hallowed, in the name of our Lord Jesus Christ." After Communion, the Bishop prayed over the newly ordained one more time saying, "Receive the Holy Ghost, whose sins you shall forgive they are forgiven them; and whose sins you shall retain, they are retained."

Finally, each of the newly ordained made his promise of obedience to the Bishop and received the kiss of peace.

The beautiful and moving ceremony was followed by a reception. Cardinal Spellman came up to greet Mrs. Capodanno, who had been afraid her wheelchair would prevent her from meeting him. The traditional first blessings were given in the seminary quadrangle. The first blessing of the newly ordained is of particular value to the faithful. Kneeling before the new priest, they would take his hands and kiss them, in an act of thanksgiving to God for the gift of the priesthood. For the newly ordained, the long line of blessings to be given was an act of gratitude for the grace of being a priest and for all the support and prayers received from family, friends, and the Catholic community during his long years of preparation.

The following day, Father Vincent celebrated his first Mass, a private one for his family and friends who had come up for the special weekend. The Mass was celebrated at the altar dedicated to the Apostles, missionaries and martyrs of the Church.

Words can never describe the feelings of a family who watch one of their own celebrate Mass for the first time. Mrs. Capodanno beamed as she saw her son take into his consecrated hands the silver chalice she had given him as an ordination gift. A simple cross and inscription on the bottom expressed their love for a husband and father present to them in spirit: "From Mom, in Memory of Pop." A chalice is the most personal and precious gift a priest owns. This chalice meant a great deal to the young missionary, who was soon to be living far away from his home and family. In his daily celebration of the Mass, it would keep his mother and all those he cherished close to his heart.

The design of Father Vincent's chalice was particularly appropriate, if not prophetic. On the node, four symbols of sacrifice took their inspiration from pagan and Christian rituals: an Indian bending over a fire; a human sacrifice; a priest offering bread; and, the summit and fulfillment of all these, a lamb bleeding into a chalice, an image of the bloodless sacrifice of Christ enacted in each Mass. The chalice illustrated the universal nature of sacrifice and atonement, and pointed dramatically to the sacrificial offering Father Vincent would make of himself in Vietnam.

At the time of Father Vincent's ordination in June of 1958, the Catholic Church was on the verge of radical changes. Pope Pius XII, then eighty-two, was in his last few months of life. By October, Angelo Cardinal Roncalli, a short, stout Venetian, would become John XXIII, and usher the Church into a new era by means of Vatican Council II.

But little of this was on the minds of Father Vincent and his classmates the day after ordination. What preoccupied them most was the American Foreign Mission Society's 41st annual departure ceremony. There, Father Vincent, along with forty-seven other young men in the class of 1958, would receive his formal mission assignment. The longing to serve in fields afar was finally to be satisfied.

The departure service began at 2:30 p.m. at the traditional Departure Bell, which is rung only once a year for this solemn occasion. The bell has a history all its own. Bishop Walsh on his first trip to the Orient was given this large bronze bell, which once had hung in a pagan temple in Japan. Since the first departure of Maryknoll missionaries in 1918, the bell has rung once a year to announce that another group is on its way to do the work of God throughout the world.

Archbishop Thomas A. Boland of Newark and Father Comber, the Superior General of Maryknoll, addressed the new missionaries who then received their assignments and their mission crucifixes. In that year's class, men were dispatched to Africa, Chile, Guatemala, Japan, Korea, Peru, the Philippines and, in Father Vincent's case, Formosa (Taiwan). The simple ceremony concluded with the singing of the "Departure Hymn," including this verse:

> Go forth, farewell for life, o dearest brothers;
> Proclaim afar the sweet name of God.
> We meet again one day in heaven's land of blessing.
> Farewell, brothers, farewell.

Just as one is greeted at Maryknoll headquarters with the *Pax Intrantibus* inscription, those who depart are given a special farewell. Inscribed on the floor near large oval doors is the Latin phrase *Salus Exeuntibus* or "Salvation to Those Who Leave."

Before leaving for the missions, Father Vincent was able to spend a little over a month with his family and ailing mother. These weeks were a time of preparation for the coming separation from them and his friends.

In accord with tradition, the new priest from Staten Island celebrated a Mass of Thanksgiving the week following ordination at his home parish of Our Lady of Good Counsel. This homecoming of sorts was an emotional occasion. Father Vincent offered the Mass with his pastor, Father Griffin — who nine years earlier had recommended him to Maryknoll — and with his good friend Father Richter, who had been ordained for the Toledo Diocese a few weeks earlier. Concelebration is a unique expression of the one priesthood of Christ in which all bishops and priests share. It was particularly meaningful to great friends such as Vincent Capodanno and William Richter, who now belonged to this unique brotherhood.

The new priest's time at home was marked by many invitations and parties. The Capodanno family enjoyed celebrating, and Father Vincent was a particularly gregarious family member — as his family has said, the life of the party. His brother James recalled, "All liked him; he was the type of fellow, that if you have a crowded room all eyes would just look up at him — no exaggeration." Father Vincent was, as well, a perfect gentleman, ever a clean and tidy dresser, especially in his new, black clerical suit. He was so neat and well groomed that there were those who speculated privately whether Father Vincent was indeed cut out for the rugged life of a missionary.

While Father Vincent busied himself with all the business and social obligations which come of an impending and extended departure, he also attended to preparing spiritually for beginning his missionary work in Formosa. His daily duty as a priest included the celebration of Mass and the saying of the Divine Office. He also read *Radiating Christ, An Appeal to Militant Catholics* by the French Jesuit, Raoul Plus. Each member of his class received this book as an ordination gift from former Rector and now Superior General, Father Comber. In a letter to Father Comber he wrote:

The ideal of the priesthood in a Maryknoller you set before us in your own life and in your conferences will always be an example to encourage me. I will strive to live up to the ideal of our Founders and ask that you help me in your prayers lest these words remain only written and not lived.

The book you gave us, *Radiating Christ*, will be a great help in directing God's light to the shadows throughout the world.

The author of *Radiating Christ* was himself a military chaplain with the French Army in World War I. For his heroism, his country awarded him the Croix de Guerre and the Medaille Militaire. After his military service, Father Plus began writing about the spiritual life, eventually authoring over forty books in which he placed special emphasis on God's loving relationship with the soul and the winning of souls for Christ. For Father Plus, the presence of God within the soul was a continual source of wonder and meditation from which he derived practical and concrete direction for those wishing to deepen their relationship with Christ and develop a closer union with Him.

What is striking about *Radiating Christ* is how this book parallels the stages of Father Vincent's own life as a missionary priest. If one genuinely wishes to understand many of the motives and sources of inspiration for Father Vincent, the reading of this spiritual work can be particularly revealing. The primary aim of the message of *Radiating Christ* is to transform a person. By closely imitating the life of Christ in an intimate way, we lose our own identity in His, allowing Christ's light and image to radiate from within us. The book asserts that we journey, like Christ, at first in a descent, then to an incarnation, a renunciation and a burial. Each of these four stages can be seen unfolding during the remaining seven and a half years of Father Vincent's life.

As the time for his departure drew near, Father Vincent cherished the few remaining days he had with his family, particularly his mother. His assignment in Taiwan would last six years, with no vacations. Rachel Capodanno's health was failing, and Father Vincent knew that this might be the last time he would see her. He arranged a short helicopter ride from Newark Airport to Idlewild Airport (now John F. Kennedy Airport), and then on to Los Angeles, so that the shock of his going so far away from his mother would be lessened. His sister Pauline remembered that he went into the restroom to cry before everyone said their final, emotional goodbye. At the same time, he bade his last farewell to close friend Father Richter. While they would continue to correspond with one another, they would never see each other again.

Nine years earlier, on his application to Maryknoll, twenty-year-old Vincent Capodanno had given his description of the life and work of a foreign missionary:

> I'll be separated from my family and friends, and all the things I'm now accustomed to, for indefinite lengths of time, during which all my efforts will be devoted to the people I'm serving. Their lives, both troubles and joys will be my life.

The moment to fulfill these words had arrived.

THE FIELD AFAR

*What is an apostle? Etymology tells us that he is
one who is sent,* missus, apostolo, *one who comes in
the name of another, who comes not to speak of himself, not to plead his own cause, but to speak of another, to plead the cause of another, another who is
understood to be greater than himself; the apostle
comes to speak of God, to plead the cause of God.*

Raoul Plus, S.J.,
Radiating Christ: An Appeal to Militant Catholics

On August 4, 1958, Father Vincent and five other Maryknoll
priests boarded the *SS Nadilee* and set out from Los Angeles to
the Orient. The other Maryknollers who had also been assigned
to Formosa were Fathers John A. Carbin, Eugene M. Murray, Joseph A. Kimmerling, Raymond H. Kelley and Don Sheehan. Father Sheehan would become Father Vincent's close friend during
their time in Taiwan. They were both assigned to the same language school in Miaoli and eventually found themselves working
in nearby missions. Though Father Sheehan had been ordained
in 1955, three years before Father Vincent, he had been asked to
do development work for Maryknoll in the United States before
receiving his first mission assignment.

The fourteen-day ocean voyage ended in Nagoya Harbor, Japan, where the missionaries had to wait out a typhoon. Father
Sheehan recalled that during their short stay in Japan, he and Father Vincent took a cab into Kyoto. The cab was exceptionally
dirty, and Father Vincent expressed some shock that the driver
relieved himself by the side of the road. This was perhaps the

first indication of what would be Father Vincent's primary struggle in Taiwan: the clash between his meticulous lifestyle and the actual conditions of the people and places he served. Father Sheehan remembered Father Vincent as "a fastidious person, a neat person; not a vulgar person; smooth, high class" — someone who might have a difficult time adjusting to an unrefined society.

After the typhoon was over, the missionaries flew from Kyoto to Taipei, the capital of Formosa.

At the very moment Father Vincent Capodanno landed in Taipei, American involvement in Southeast Asia was evolving dramatically. Subsequent events in Vietnam would grow from the policies decided upon during this period.

Following World War II, the United States remained deeply committed to the defense of free nations and kept a watchful eye on Communist advances in the Orient. The United States recognized Chiang Kai-shek's Nationalist Republic of China in Taiwan as the only legitimate Chinese government — temporarily in exile. In summer 1958, when the Communist Chinese made a play to annex the territory of the island groups Quemoy and Matsu, Secretary of State John Foster Dulles set forth what was known as "The Formosa Doctrine," recognizing the security and protection of Quemoy and Matsu as related to the defense of Taiwan, and hence, to the preservation of democracy in the East. In his inaugural address of January 20, 1961, President Kennedy explicitly laid down the principle that would guide America's involvement in Southeast Asia: "We shall pay any price, bear any burden, meet any hardship, support any friend, oppose any foe to assure the survival and success of liberty." The gauntlet had been thrown. America had taken her stand.

Taiwan has traditionally been a place of refuge. With mainland China only 100 miles to the east across the Formosa straight, people have been coming to her for centuries to escape political storms, disgruntled mandarins and merchants, changing imperial parties, and most recently Communism.

Taiwans strategic location as stepping stone from the mainland to the Pacific has meant occupation by both European and Asian forces. The Portuguese arrived first in 1590, designating the area "Ilha Formosa," or "Beautiful Island." They were later expelled by the Spanish and Dutch. For a while, the great Tai-wanese hero Koxinga made Taiwan an independent entity, but his rule eventually fell to the Manchurians. After the Sino-Japa-nese War in 1895, Taiwan passed into the hands of the Japanese who held it until the end of World War II, leaving behind them many marks of Japanese culture and language. After the Com-munist takeover of the mainland in the late forties, Nationalist leader Chiang Kai-shek chose Taipei in Taiwan as the capital of the Republic of China.

The people of Taiwan fall into several main groups compris-ing the aborigines and the descendants of successive waves of immigration from the Chinese mainland.

Fathers Capodanno and Sheehan were sent to work with the Hakka-Chinese living in the municipality of Miaoli, located on the west coast of Taiwan about seventy miles south of Taipei. In ancient times, the Hakka had been a persecuted minority group in the Kwangtung Mountains of Northern China. Pushed further and further south, they were gradually forced off the mainland and into western and inland Formosa. The Hakka, literally "guests" or "strangers," are one of Taiwan's most enterprising peoples: proud and intelligent, they posses their own distinct lan-guage and customs. About 10 percent of the population of Tai-wan speak the Hakka dialect.

The Hakka had to their honor the witness of a great Maryknoller, Bishop Francis Xavier Ford, who had lived and worked among them. The inspiring example of Bishop Ford must have gained a profound dimension for Father Vincent as he grew to know and love the Hakka people his predecessor had served.

Without a doubt, Maryknoll was greatly responsible for the diffusion of the Catholic Faith in Formosa. The first Catholic missionaries to arrive on the island were Spanish Dominicans in the 17th century, but with the loss of Formosa to the Dutch, and subse-quently, Protestant Dutch missionaries, the Catholic mission field dwindled. In 1949, however, as priests, religious and lay people were expelled by the Communists from mainland China, the Catho-lic population of Taiwan grew at an amazing rate. Within fifteen years there would be a tenfold increase in the number of Catholics on the island. Many of these were Maryknoll missionaries, often arriving with their entire congregation in tow.

Father Vincent must have felt somewhat at home on Taiwan. There were many elements of the island's persona which were similar to his family's origins on the Mediterranean coast. For one thing, the dramatic tension between the beauty of the land and the almost daily earthquakes harkens back to the volcanic activity within sight of scenic Sorrento. But most especially, Father Vincent would have understood and appreciated how the family acts as the most important element in traditional Taiwanese society. Deriving from the precepts of Confucianism, filial piety and ancestor worship are the primary virtues. The Taiwanese are a profoundly religious people, practicing a mix of Buddhism and Taoism, seeing in everything a spiritual dimension. This religious orientation and respect for ancestry were quite familiar to the young Italian-American missionary.

Immediately upon arrival in Taipei, Fathers Capodanno and Sheehan were taken to the Bishop's residence in the city of Miaoli. Bishop Frederick A. Donaghy was the Dean of Miaoli and the Regional Superior for Maryknoll. Originally from Bedford, Massachusetts, he had been made a bishop in 1940, one of the youngest bishops in the world at that time. He was known for his humor and hospitality, which he now lavished upon his recently arrived brothers. Bishop Donaghy had stood up bravely in the face of beatings and interrogations at the hands of the Communists in China during the early fifties. No doubt he shared these stories with his young guests who were just beginning their ministry and might be called upon to give equally heroic witness.

Though it would take some time for the new missionaries to adjust to the culture, food and subtropical climate of Formosa — not to mention the occasional tremors — they had to start laying the foundation for their future activities. Within a few days of their arrival, Father Donald McGinnis drove them to their new home, the language school in Miaoli.

The school was built in the middle of a compound, surrounded by a customary brick wall with broken glass set in concrete on the top for security. The main house was built in the

Japanese style with a garden in the middle and sliding screen doors separating the rooms. Father Sheehan's room was on the right of the main entrance and Father Vincent's on the left. Their beds were equipped with the indispensable mosquito netting.

The priest in charge of their formation and education at the language school was Father Charles Hilbert, an old "China hand," the name given to any Maryknoller who had been expelled from China by the Communists. Father Hilbert, who had taught himself to read and speak Hakka, would oversee the education of the two young missionaries in the Hakka language for the next ten months.

Fathers Capodanno and Sheehan were encouraged in their efforts by the obvious accomplishment of their teacher, Father Hilbert. Every morning, after Mass and spiritual exercises, Father Hilbert would spend an hour going over the lesson for the day. A young Hakka student from town who knew a little English was hired to spend the morning and early afternoon going over the simple lessons which were taken from old, handwritten texts that were smuggled from China — the only known primers which explained the intricate Hakka dialect. Instruction consisted of the constant repetition of the sounds and tones that distinguish one Chinese word from the next. The exhausting and tedious program was necessary if the two men were to become effective missionaries.

In their leisure hours, the two new missionaries spent their time together and would often visit Father McGinnis who, while older, was still not considered an old timer. On Wednesday afternoons, they would go to the theater in downtown Miaoli. Father Sheehan recalled that on their first visit to the theater, Father Vincent was amazed at the dirt floor and the dank air filled with the smoke of homemade Chinese cigarettes. Curious children would come up to Father Vincent to run their filthy hands over his hairy arms, an unusual sight in the Orient. Both priests would spend part of their thirty-dollar monthly stipend on Winston cigarettes available on the black market.

The missionaries also enjoyed riding their bikes and motor scooters through the two-mile stretch of town. Between classroom work and life on the streets of Miaoli, the two priests gradually picked up the Hakka language. The two of them always got a laugh when they heard one of the Hakkas utter their favorite Chinese expression: "A perfectly happy person lives in America, marries a Japanese wife, and eats Chinese food."

All Maryknollers of the time were quite concerned when officials of the People's Republic of China relentlessly interrogated Bishop James Edward Walsh. Bishop Walsh, who was known by the people he served as "the pillar of truth," was sentenced in March 1961 to twenty years in a Chinese prison. Bishop Walsh's suffering showcased the agonies of many who suffered at the hands of the Communists. The accounts of torture and hatred of missionaries and Christian Chinese are amply documented in Bill Surface and Jim Hart's book *Freedom Bridge*.

> Chinese Communist leader Mao Tse-tung publicly divided the world into The People' and 'The Enemy,' and Christians were the enemy. . . . Missioners, especially on Northern China, were known to have been undressed, given kangaroo trials, then buried or boiled alive or stomped to death for their 'crimes.' Catechists were rolled in beds of broken glass, or pushed into river ice holes until they were drowned or frozen. Seminary students near Peking were nailed hand and foot to two-wheeled carts pulled by horses which lashed into full gallop over rough roads. Then the executioners slit the boys' chests and cut out their hearts, which they strung on reeds for exhibition.

The stories of torture and martyrdom were well known by all missionaries and those who read *The Field Afar*. Like his colleagues, Father Vincent was ready to stand as a Christian witness on behalf of the Gospel.

The language school ended in June 1959. For ten months Father Vincent had struggled with the Hakka language but failed to reach the same level of proficiency as his friend Father Sheehan. He continued to have difficulty forming the aspirate sounds that are essential to speaking the dialect. Even after years in Taiwan, he never really grasped the language and this failure disappointed him. On the other hand, perhaps unknown to Father Vincent, his problems speaking the language contributed to his formation as an attentive listener who found simple ways of expressing his ideas. Later, in Vietnam, he would attract the confidence of young Marines partly because of his unique capacity to hear what they said — and didn't say — and respond to it with sympathy and sincerity.

Following a short vacation, the two priests were assigned to their missionary territories. Father Vincent went to a Hakka plains parish in a tiny village called Tunglo. His pastor, Father Maynard Murphy, was a lot like Capodanno: both liked clean waxed floors and an orderly rectory. Father Vincent fit in quite well there. In contrast, Father Sheehan was sent to Tahu, where struggles with the rather unstructured style of the pastor finally lead him to another parish in San Wan, close to Father Vincent.

Father Vincent was now truly "in the field." Finishing the language course did not mean the end of his education in Hakka — he would pass many an evening in solitude writing and then diligently translating his sermons into the Hakka dialect — but it was the end of the official Maryknoll program that produces the missionary. He was now serving in the ordinary, daily duties of a Maryknoll priest. The dream was now a reality, and as in most cases, reality is very different from the dream.

The daily life for a missionary in Taiwan was as unstructured as seminary life was structured. Each priest had to evaluate on a daily basis what needed to be done and how best to do it. He had to be a self-starter with a creative bent. The discipline and training of those seminary years came in as an important asset in the mountain village.

In addition to distributing relief food and medicine, Father Vincent's duties included teaching native catechists so that they, in turn, could go into the villages and catechize the populace. Ever since the pontificate of Pius XI, the need and importance of native clergy and catechists was an uppermost consideration for missionaries. Father Vincent would go to the villages to offer support to the catechists, following up their teaching work with the celebration of the sacraments, especially Baptism.

The missionaries went by the title "shen fu," which means "spiritual father." The challenges of life in Taiwan were much different from those faced by the earlier missionaries in China and Korea, where imprisonment or death was often the result of missionary life. This was the reward that Bishop Walsh was then living and would continue to endure until July 1970 when he was unexpectedly and without explanation released from prison. For the most part, Taiwan was at peace, and the people were generally receptive to the message of the Gospel.

For Father Vincent the greatest challenge to missionary life may have been the living conditions. He must have enjoyed the respite of his periodic vacations to Japan and Hong Kong. In Hong Kong, visiting Maryknollers would stay at "Stanley House," which always provided a clean and welcome change from the poor and sometimes unsanitary conditions in Formosa. Father Paul Brien, a fellow missionary in Taiwan, remembered, "Vince did not like dirt, he always kept himself orderly and spic and span; while he was a good missioner, it is my hunch that the mountain assignment was difficult for this reason." Father McGinnis, who knew Father Vincent quite well, noted, "He did not fit the 'missioner mystique' of being a rough-and-ready priest. Instead, Father Vincent was clean cut and proper; his shoes were always shined — something hard to accomplish in the mountains." Even Bishop Donaghy noted that Father Vincent was rather meticulous in dress, but felt he would adapt himself to conditions of a missionary.

In fact, Father Vincent was learning the first lesson on the spiritual journey: humility. He was a good, solid priest; but he was a perfectionist. He liked things done right. He probably felt self-conscious about being so systematic when his colleagues were so spontaneous and carefree. He very likely had days when he questioned his position and usefulness as a missionary in the loosely organized missions of Taiwan. All this was compounded by his difficulty with the language, contributing to a sense of being isolated, alone, and misunderstood.

When the Maryknoll General Superior gave the newly ordained copies of *Radiating Christ,* he must have known that they would each face their moment of descent when they would have to accept their limitations and depend fully on Christ. How striking are the opening words of *Radiating Christ* when placed in this context: "The winning of souls calls in the first place for humility: descent. The first virtue that the apostle must have if he would influence his contemporaries is disinterestedness."

One of Father Vincent's greatest sources of strength and pleasure was his on-going correspondence with family and friends. While only a few letters have survived from when he was in Taiwan, his family recalls many letters and tapes from him. He always remembered birthdays and was quick to send a thank you note for a gift received. He especially wrote to his mother and managed to call her on her birthday every year.

In one letter to his sister Pauline and her family, he itemized a list of "thank you's" for all that they had done for him. He went on in the newsy letter to write about the traditions of the Chinese New Year in his village:

> Even Tunglo had a dragon parade! We contributed thirty TN (ninety cents U.S.) towards the making of the dragon and since that was the largest contribution in Tunglo we got a special bow as the dragon went past last night. . . . usually the dragon first goes to the pagan temple and worships the idols. I had to make sure the Tunglo dragon was just going thru the streets before I gave the money. The boys who were going to carry it said 'No temple for us' and I don't think they did go.

On February 27, 1961, Rachel Capodanno, the seventy-two-year-old family matriarch, passed away. She had been a widow for nearly a quarter century and, in that time, her faith and strength of character had guided the family through good times and bad. Father Vincent's brothers and sisters wanted to fly him home for the funeral, but Maryknoll's policy would not allow him to leave. The young missionary was obedient without hesitation, although he no doubt longed to be with his family. He painfully recalled his mother's worries and resistance at the time of his entrance into Maryknoll because he would be living in a foreign country, far removed from her final years and even her death.

Father Vincent's deep, spiritual love for his mother, and his Christian thoughts on death, are evident in a very revealing letter he wrote to his sister Mary. He said, in part:

> Mom's death certainly came as a shock to all of us. Mom's letters in the recent past contained no certain indications she felt her health was failing badly. . . .

In many ways, Mary, we have much to be thankful for: it would have been very hard on Mom if she had to be confined to bed, and still not find any real relief from the pain. . . . Her death was sudden, yes; but her whole life of praying and making so many sacrifices prepared her well.

We haven't really lost Mom. Now, in Heaven, she can be with us all and not be away from any of us. How happy that must make Mom. . . .

For us, we have the many beautiful memories of Mom to sustain us until that time when we all, Mom and Pop and all of us, are united permanently in Heaven.

The ignorance, fear and hopelessness with which pagans face death must indeed by a terrifying thing to have to go thru life with. Keep them in your prayers that our work here and in all parts of the world will bring them to a knowledge of God and ultimately to eternal happiness, such as we can have for the asking.

In the fall of 1960, Father Vincent was assigned to the mountain village of Ching An in the township of Tai An as the director of a youth hostel for boys of high school age. The young Chinese men spent a year at the hostel in preparation for the national college entrance exam. The pressure to do well on the exam and the intense competition it created led some to extreme depression and even to suicide.

The hostel, formally a police barracks, was opened by Father Vincent and started with ten young Catholic men. His job was to meet their spiritual needs, counsel them through the difficult examinations, and try to instill Christian values in these future leaders of Taiwan. He would have been able to empathize very well with their academic struggles, never having been himself a great scholar and even then still struggling with their language. It's clear that he had a gift of ministry with young men, particularly those facing difficult trials. Friends and associates are consistent in describing him as soft spoken and a good listener, someone who made them feel he was with them in their suffering.

Father Vincent's time at the Hostel was not without its comic side. Father Richter recounts, "His youth hospice was next door to a Buddhist Temple which had many funerals, complete with a band whose favorite song was: 'I wonder whose [sic] kissing her now?' played as a funeral dirge, very slowly and solemnly, over and over, many times a day."

From this point on, we begin to see in Father Vincent's life what *Radiating Christ* describes as the "Incarnation." Strictly speaking, this word refers to faith in the God-man, Jesus Christ. For the disciple of Christ, however, incarnation also means making Christ visible again to the world in his own person, by his words, but most importantly, by his example. The apostle is to attract others to himself with his love, warmth, good humor and a welcoming heart. He is to be all things to all men to draw them back to their Father in heaven through the Word made flesh who came to save them.

To live Christ Jesus was the greatest desire of Father Vincent's heart. From the start, he was attracted to Maryknoll because he saw in the life of the missionary the fullest realization of this desire. In the words of co-founder Bishop James A. Walsh:

> There is a spirit which is one of the striking features of Maryknoll — a spirit which I like to call a joyous restraint, and a peace born of a common desire to sacrifice all for God. . . . Its summation is *charity* — the love of God and the love of neighbor for God.

Father Vincent held several other assignments during his six years in Taiwan. In 1961, after his appointment at the youth hostel, he became the acting pastor of Holy Rosary parish in North Miaoli. In 1962, Father returned to Tunglo as Father Maynard Murphy's associate pastor. In 1963, he was given his final assignment as pastor of a parish in Ch'ng An.

With his six-year mission assignment completed, Father Vincent received the traditional six-month furlough. Classmate Father Dick Murto, who had just finished his own missionary assignment in Japan, accompanied Father Vincent to the Holy Land. It was a great grace to visit these holy places, to walk in the footsteps of the Lord, to feel the concreteness of the faith in time and space. Father Vincent visited all the places associated with Christ's passion, death, and resurrection: the way of the cross, Golgatha, the empty tomb. Two years later, during Holy Week, just three days before Easter, Father Vincent would begin his own way of the cross when he arrived in Da Nang, Vietnam.

In October 1964, Father Vincent returned home to the United States. He stayed with his sister Pauline and her family at their house in Kearny, New Jersey. He spent most of his short stay attending numerous homecoming parties. He also accepted the invitation to say Mass at the local church.

During his time at home, Father Vincent's brother James helped him re-learn driving a car. He had gotten out of practice in Taiwan where a motor scooter and a bicycle sufficed for transportation. James took him out to practice on Seaside Boulevard which, only ten years after these lessons, would be renamed Father Capodanno Boulevard.

Anyone who has ever left the United States for a few years knows the odd sensation of returning. Even coming from a close-knit, Italian-American family, Vincent Capodanno was an American, with the characteristic values of an American. For six years he had been among another people whose values were quite different; he had made the difficult transition to another way of living. It must have been a bit of "home-culture shock," to once again be surrounded by such material prosperity, pragmatic thinking, and individualism. How must New York Harbor and the old ride on the Staten Island Ferry have looked to him after seeing Hong Kong harbor? How must it have felt to sit down to a plentiful table or walk through the grocery store after having seen the shortages of food in Taiwan? How must it have been to hear people complain about tempests in teapots after living with men who had faced imprisonment and death under Communism?

Father Vincent did not realize it, but the six-month furlough, he was enjoying was actually the calm before the storm. Profound changes were about to take place in his life. In these changes the Holy Spirit was going to enable him to radiate Christ in ways he never could have imagined.

In March 1965, Father Vincent returned to Taiwan only to be informed that he had been reassigned to the Maryknoll Fathers' School in Hong Kong. He was astounded and dismayed by the news.

A change of assignments and countries is an unusual move for a mission society, the norm being that a missionary spend his life ministering to the people he was first sent to serve. The missionary participates in a kind of incarnation, becoming one with his people, drawing always closer to them in language and culture, understanding more and more their needs and how he can best meet them. According to Father McGinnis, a change of assignment such as Father Vincent was being asked to make would be "jarring," a big switch. The language spoken in Hong Kong is Cantonese and not Hakka. To go to Hong Kong was tantamount to losing six years dedicated work and beginning from scratch.

According to notes of a meeting of Maryknoll priests in Miaoli, Father Vincent was transferred to Hong Kong to compensate for a lack of manpower in that area. Personnel changes were imminent: at least one priest was out due to illness; others were soon to go on furlough. The need for a replacement priest was urgent. Father Brien expected Father Vincent would like the assignment because it seemed to fit his lifestyle more than any other kind of work in Taiwan. Commenting on Father Vincent's time in Taiwan, Father Brien noted, "Vince was a good missioner . . . but I do think he had a difficulty when he was in the mountains." He thought Father Vincent was struggling with less than ideal conditions and frustrated by his inability to master the language. The opinion that Father Vincent's transfer flowed directly from his problems with the Hakka dialect was shared by Father Sheehan as well.

At the heart of the matter may have been personality conflicts. Father John Rich, then stationed in the Philippines but still in contact with Father Vincent, remarked, "Taiwan was not healthy for him; he felt that what he wanted to do was not acceptable and that the superiors . . . were not hearing what he wanted to do or what his needs were." A letter from Father Vincent to the Vicar General of Maryknoll, Father John F. Donovan, indicated that the young priest may indeed have had a problem with his superiors in Taiwan; this may have prompted them to recommend a change. Relations between Bishop Donaghy and Father Vincent were strained. During his recently completed furlough in the States he had met with Bishop Donaghy and expressed his strong desire to remain in Taiwan. Now he was being transferred.

Whatever the reason, the period was one of deep personal pain and anxiety for Father Vincent. He must have felt that he had fallen into a great darkness. Yet, grace was at work in him in a profound way, manifesting itself perhaps as darkness, pain, and confusion, but purifying his intentions and making of him the priest and the man he always hoped to be.

To his family, however, Father Vincent revealed little of his ordeal. A letter home shows him focusing on the positive reasons for this transfer:

> I am being transferred to Hong Kong to teach at the Maryknoll Fathers' School there. Several of the men there are due for furlough, some are being changed to assignments in the U.S. and one or more is sick. I was the only free person around so all factors rolled into one fact: I go to Hong Kong. It may be temporary or permanent depending on various people getting well or back to the school. It will be very interesting and I'll have much to write and say after I am there. I will also study some Cantonese, but that I have to arrange for after I settle down to teaching and a class schedule.

Father Vincent arrived in Hong Kong on March 21, 1965, in the middle of the high school semester. As soon as he arrived he began a campaign to return to his old post. His first written request for transfer was made on April 1. Five days later, Bishop Donaghy denied his request. Persistent, Father Vincent wrote another letter on April 9 asking to be relieved of all duties so he could study the Chinese language. Once again, on April 21, Bishop Donaghy denied his request, stating that Father Vincent was needed more to teach than to study Cantonese. However, three weeks later the Bishop had a change of heart and informed Father Vincent that he could enroll for a one-year course at the New Asia College.

Seeing this permission as perhaps an indication that the Bishop could be persuaded further, Father Vincent wrote once again asking to be reassigned to Taiwan. He said:

I cannot sit by and watch as that period of time is written off as a total loss. Those six years can be at least salvaged partially by arranging for the use of the experience acquired during them. I therefore ask once more to be sent to Taichung.

In his frustration, Father Vincent wrote directly to Bishop Comber, making clear his desire to leave Hong Kong. The letter, dated June 3, stated: "For reasons of health, as mentioned in the physician's note enclosed herein, I respectfully request to be transferred from the Taiwan-Hong Kong Region to another mission Region."

Bishop Comber's two replies to Father Vincent show us that the younger missionary was not at all satisfied with certain aspects of his assignments. The Bishop's first letter, dated June 8, said:

> We don't want to take you from Taiwan Region if it is at all possible for you to work there. You have studied the language there, and you have the ability to succeed as a good missioner. The doctor's letter seems to indicate that you have a nervous condition. This is something that someone might get in any place in the world and could be of a passing nature. You don't want to make a decision that affects your entire career too quickly. At the same time, I want to emphasize that we wish to help you in every way possible.

The Bishop continued to express his concern in a July 8 letter:

> I know that studying new languages is not easy. I also know that you were unhappy with some of the situations in Miaoli. These are not things, however, that should make you decide to leave the Region. No matter what region or mission that you are in, there will be difficult moments. Your vocation is to be a missioner and learn to live with some disappointments.

His superior's direction was firm and clear, but Father Vincent continued to explore various options. The surface difficulties — language, personality differences, love of cleanliness and order — all this cannot fully explain what was happening in the man. He was laboring under a profound restlessness — a clamor similar to the one he felt when he first was called to priesthood. It is very difficult to know if such a state comes from God, or from an unwillingness to fully obey those who have legitimate authority. What is remarkable is that Father Vincent lived out this arduous time of discernment without ever defying his superiors. Although insistent in his requests, he remained obedient. Within the context of obedience, and not outside it, he grew not only in relation to his superiors, but to the prompting of the Holy Spirit within his own heart. This is true humility, the true emptying out of the self, the true descent, and the first step towards a true incarnation.

In early July, Bishop Comber received an amazing cablegram from Father Vincent:

> AS FULFILLMENT OF PERSONAL DESIRE AND HELP FILL DIRE NEED RESPECTFULLY REQUEST PERMISSION TO JOIN NAVY CHAPLAINS HOPEFULLY WAITING PERMISSION AND YOUR GOOD WISHES

Bishop Comber replied immediately, and with some concern, to Father Vincent's request. He said, "I am not particularly adverse to your entering the Navy, but I do think you should take your time about such a decision." He suggested that unhappiness should not prompt a hasty choice.

But Father Vincent was wasting no time in forging ahead with his plans. Obviously the idea had come to him as a burst of light — the solution to a badly needed change. He seized on it with all the conviction of his passionate nature. In July 1965 he wrote to the Chief of Chaplains in Washington, D.C., inquiring about the possibility of joining the Navy Chaplain Corps, and revealing his particular desire to serve with the Marines in Vietnam:

1 I would like to join the Navy with the intention of serving as a chaplain to the Marine Corps. Is this possible? [The Navy Chaplain Corps serves Navy, Marine and Coast Guard units.]

2 May I volunteer specifically for immediate duty in Vietnam?

3 Where and how long is Chaplain's training school?

4 What is the minimum term of enlistment?

On August 9, 1965, Father Vincent wrote the Bishop one last letter explaining his frustration and seeking permission to join the Navy. He explained:

> After having been refused four times to be transferred from Hong Kong to Taichung, I considered it improper to make the same request of you and unlikely that you would grant it even if I did make it and therefore wrote requesting to be transferred to a different Region.
>
> After receiving your replies of June 8 and July 8, I then requested to join the Chaplain Corps. I felt and do feel that this request, which would keep me in the Society where I wish to remain and yet would effect a necessary change, provide the most personally desirable work arrangement.

Why did Father Vincent want to join the military and serve specifically with the Marines in Vietnam? Why was he unsatisfied with his assignments in Taiwan and Hong Kong? The answer to these questions brings us close to the heart of Father Vincent Capodanno.

His request to serve in the military was not without precedent. He knew other Maryknoll priests who served with the armed forces, finding it a very rewarding and challenging way of missionary life. He knew the stories of famous Maryknoll missionaries who had served as chaplains; men like Father Joseph Sweeney, the first Maryknoller to volunteer to be a chaplain in World War II. After the invading Japanese had forced Father Sweeney from his leper colony in Japan, he joined the Air Force as a chaplain for the duration of the war. As soon as the war was over, he went back to China to begin work with the lepers again until the Communist Chinese finally drove him out for good in 1953.

Another Maryknoller who served as a chaplain in World War II was also one of the most famous chaplains of all time. Father William T. Cummings had been sent as a missionary to the Philippines in the forties. When the war broke out, he went to the Army's headquarters in Manila and asked to help the young soldiers. He said, "I want to get into the Army. I don't care whether I get a commission or not. I don't care whether I have a uniform or a place to sleep. But the boys will be needing priests, and I want to help them." His request was granted.

During the bombing of a hospital, Father Cummings kept the injured men calm by praying with them. He stayed with his men even after a bomb exploded near him, breaking his arm and cutting his shoulder. Despite his wound, and a doctor's plea for him to rest, he went to help the men at the front lines, arguing, "Doc, there are a lot of men up front far worse off than I am. I'm going up to help them." At the front he was captured and forced to endure the horrific Bataan Death March. He finally met his death as a prisoner of war aboard a ship en route to Japan from the Philippines. He was always known to be cheerful, even to the end of his life. Father Cummings coined the timeless phrase, "There are no atheists in foxholes."

When Father Vincent arrived in Formosa the memory of Father Cummings was still very much alive. Like Father Cummings, Father Vincent would seek to minister to that vibrant faith born in the front line of action; he would bring cheerfulness and peace to the men under his care.

Pauline Capodanno Costa suggested that the reason her brother wanted to serve as a chaplain was rooted in his profound desire to be where he was needed. "He wasn't pro-war or anything, but he was very concerned about the American troops over there. He already knew the language and knew he could help." Father Vincent's own words lend credence to this opinion. In October 1966, a reporter in Vietnam asked him why he became a chaplain, and he answered, "I joined the Chaplain Corps when the Vietnam War broke out because I think I'm needed here as are many more chaplains. I'm glad to help in the way I can."

Father Vincent seemed to be compelled by two factors to join the Marines and serve in Vietnam. First, he wanted to go where he was needed. One of the founders of Maryknoll had defined a missionary as "One who goes where he is needed but not wanted; and stays until he is wanted but not needed." Father Vincent felt he was no longer needed in Hong Kong or Taiwan as much as he would be in Vietnam.

The second reason was a desire to change his life, to find an assignment that would force him to go deeper as a priest and a missionary. From his older brother James, who served with the Marines during World War II, he no doubt learned of the spirit and dedication for which the Marines are famous. The Marine Corps is arguably the most difficult and demanding of the military services, as their slogan "first to fight" expresses. Being a Marine chaplain in Vietnam would definitely challenge the very core of Father Vincent's priesthood and his role as missionary. He was drawn to the cutting edge where he would be not just a Catholic priest, but a missionary; not just a missionary, but a military chaplain; not just a military chaplain, but a Marine.

Yet Father Vincent's fellow missionaries in Taiwan, and his classmate Father Rich in the Philippines, could not picture him as a military chaplain. Father Rich commented that while it was not unusual for a priest to request to become a military chaplain, it seemed odd that Father Vincent would choose this way of life. Father McGinnis was taken aback also, knowing the rough and muddy life of the Marines — certainly more rugged than the conditions of the mountainous Hakka village. He couldn't understand Father Vincent's desire to be one of them. Father Sheehan, who would later follow suit and become an Air Force chaplain in Vietnam, recalled, "What most impressed me about him is that he is the last person in the world I thought would be a Marine chaplain. Navy chaplain I could see: spic and span, everything in order on a ship. It blew my mind to learn he was a real grunt."

But the most interesting remark, and by far the most insightful, was that of Father Brien: "Most guys here were surprised when Vince joined the Marines. I don't think any of us really saw him as that kind of person. Being a Marine and being a grunt, heroism and warfare seemed to be the opposite side of Vince that most people did not know. I guess we really did not know Vince."

It does seem that despite a warm and socially gregarious nature, Vincent Capodanno tended to be reticent about the deepest things in his heart. Perhaps this was the result of growing up the youngest in an Italian-American family where the level of interpersonal involvement is very high and privacy is sometimes hard to find. It's interesting that he never mentioned to his family his inclinations to the priesthood. Nor did he fully reveal to them what he was going through during his transfer to Hong Kong.

But another explanation would follow the theology of *Radiating Christ*. Perhaps Father Vincent really was a different man after six years in Taiwan. Perhaps he had arrived at that surrender, that descent which makes possible what is humanly out of reach. The thirst of Christ for souls becomes the thirst of the disciple. The disciple is seized by a desire to change his life — but this is difficult to do where people know you and expect a certain behavior from you. New wine needs new wineskins. The job had to reflect the immensity of the desire.

On August 13, 1965, Bishop Comber consented to Father Vincent's request, giving him permission to transfer to Hawaii and begin the process of military induction. Father Vincent wrote to Bishop Comber immediately and excitedly to inform him of his plans:

> I shall enlist in the Navy with the stated request and intention of serving as chaplain in the Marine Corps who use Navy men since they have no chaplains of their own. I hope to be able to volunteer for immediate duty in Vietnam, which, according to the Marine Liaison Officer at the American Consulate here, may very likely be granted.

Father Vincent was re-energized by this new assignment. He was inspired by a renewed sense of purpose and pastoral mission. His spirituality blossomed as he let himself be lead towards a deeper experience of the Incarnation. To take that step he had to once again let go of the familiar and strike out into unknown territory; but it was a step he had to make to be faithful to himself and his vocation. In the end, Father Vincent Capodanno was more a priest, more a missionary, and more a man because he was true to what he had in his heart. He exemplified what the Old Testament reveals as the fundamental attribute of God as Father: fidelity. He would find himself at home with men who lived by the words "Semper Fidelis."

ST. MARTIN'S CLOAK

Saving the world has never been an easy task. It was not easy for the Son of God. It was not easy for His Apostles. But He is with us. And that brings us back to the confidence of our beginning. Under such a leader, is there any limit to what soldiers may do, soldiers full of zeal and resolution, trained in His methods?

Raoul Plus, S.J.,
Radiating Christ: An Appeal to Militant Catholics

Father Vincent Capodanno's new career as a chaplain in the United States Navy placed him within a long and honorable tradition which extended as far back as Ancient Rome. In fact, the word "chaplain" derives from the Latin word for cloak; it was the cloak of an early Christian saint which became for all time the symbol of brotherly love manifested by the men who serve as chaplains.

As the story goes, Martin of Tours began his career as a soldier for Caesar and ended his life as a soldier for Christ. He was born around the year 315, the son of a pagan army officer, and at the age of fifteen was inducted into the army against his will. Sometime around the year 337, while stationed at Amiens, France, Martin came upon a poorly clad beggar freezing to death in the bitter cold. Feeling compassion for the unfortunate man, he drew his sword and divided his own cloak in two, giving half of it to the beggar. Later that night, Christ came to Martin in a dream, dressed in his half cloak. Martin converted to Christianity and, refusing to fight, received his discharge from the military.

The virtues of the soldier stayed with Martin as he gave heroic witness against the Arian heresy. Many great men and scholars fell prey to this pernicious teaching which sought to deny the divinity of Christ. For the Arians, Christ's humanity was a true stumbling block: how could God become a man? Instead of accepting the full implication of the Incarnation, the Arians held Christ to be merely a creature and, in so doing, they denied the fundamental tenet of the Christian faith.

In defense of the Gospel, Martin suffered scourging and exile; yet he was known for his extraordinary compassion to enemies, even intervening to prevent the execution of heretics whom he had publicly opposed. He finally settled in France where he founded the first monastic community in that area and, ten years later, despite his objections, he was made Bishop of Tours. He died in 397 and his tomb became a favorite shrine of pilgrims in the Middle Ages.

The courage and compassion of Saint Martin is a cornerstone in the history of the chaplaincy. A relic of his famous cloak was preserved by the kings of France and carried with their armies when they went to war. On the field, it was placed in a tent and cared for by the cappellani, the chaplains, who also saw to the spiritual needs of the king and his men.

In the United States, the history of the chaplain corps began in the same moment that the colonies put together a standing army in defense of their freedom. The second article of Navy regulations adopted by the Continental Congress in 1775 read: "The commanders of the ships of the Thirteen United Colonies are to take care that divine service be performed twice a day on board, and a sermon preached on Sundays, unless bad weather or other extraordinary accidents prevent."

John Paul Jones, naval hero of the American Revolution, also saw the importance of chaplains and sought two for positions on his ships, the *Ranger* and the *Bonhomme Richard*. Admiral Jones listed the requirements of a chaplain as:

> A man of reading and of letters whose sanctity of manners and happy principles would diffuse unanimity and cheerfulness thro' the ship. Such a man would necessarily be worthy [of] the

highest confidence, and might, therefore, assure himself of my esteem and friendship, and always have a place at my table.

Roman Catholic priests have served as chaplains in each branch of the Armed Forces. The first priest known to have served in the Navy was Father Adam Marshall, a Jesuit, who was listed as a schoolmaster aboard the *USS North Carolina* in 1824.

Another Jesuit, Father Anthony Rey, who served under General Zachary Taylor during the Mexican War in 1846, was the first priest to be killed during his military service. Father Rey was known for his bravery in battle, frequently exposing himself to enemy fire in order to minister to the wounded and dying soldiers. His brotherly love extended also to the natives of the area. Against the advice of his fellow officers, he went to preach a mission to the locals but in so doing was murdered by guerillas. In Father Rey we see exemplified two perennial characteristics of the chaplain: fidelity to the soldiers in his care, and a sincere charity for all men, seeing even in the "enemy" a child of God.

Catholic chaplains provided solace to both the Union and Confederate armies during the Civil War. Perhaps the best known of these was Father William Corby, CSC, who served as chaplain of the Union Army's famous Irish Brigade, and who later became president of Notre Dame University. In 1888, Father Charles Henry Parks of the Archdiocese of New York became the first priest to be fully commissioned an officer in the Navy. The same year, Pope Pius IX granted Archbishop Michael Augustine Corrigan of the New York Archdiocese special faculties to appoint new chaplains.

Though Catholic priests were serving regularly with the Armed Forces, there did not exist as yet a central office to oversee their recruitment and activity. The great need for Catholic chaplains during World War I prompted the Holy See to create a special diocese for the men and women of the United States armed forces and their civilian assistants. Although the term "diocese" usually refers to territory, in the case of the military, it refers to the persons under the bishop's care. Since a bishop is also called an ordinary, the term Military Ordinariate is used when speaking of this special diocese.

In 1917, the Archdiocese of New York, the home of the Capodanno family, was chosen as the seat of the new Military Ordinariate, with a section in Washington working directly with the Armed Forces. The Holy See appointed Auxiliary Bishop Patrick J. Hayes the first Military Ordinary of the United States Army and Navy chaplains. Under Bishop Hayes's jurisdiction were the Armed Forces of the United States at home and abroad, as well as associated groups of civilians — roughly one million people. Hayes so effectively recruited and organized the corps of Catholic chaplains that by the end of the war in November of 1918 there were 1,523 priests deployed in five geographical areas called vicariates. The eighty-seven priests from New York formed a contingent more than twice as large as that from any other diocese.

Francis Cardinal Spellman followed Hayes as Archbishop of New York and Military Ordinary. During World War II, he directed the activities of more than 5,000 Catholic chaplains. Their contribution was impressive: by the end of the war, Catholic chaplains had received 832 decorations and citations for bravery. Seventy-six priests gave the ultimate sacrifice of their lives. Cardinal Spellman himself became a familiar figure during his frequent visits to military bases around the world, a practice that he continued after the war, endearing him to the hearts of American service personnel everywhere.

In 1985, Pope John Paul II created the Archdiocese for Military Services and appointed Joseph Ryan its first Archbishop. Archbishop Edwin O'Brien, who once served as a chaplain in Vietnam, now heads the Archdiocese.

The Marine Corps, though existing as a specific branch of the Armed Forces of the United States, relies on the Navy for its chaplains and medical personnel. The first Navy chaplain to serve with the Marines was J. F. Fleming, who cared for the First Provisional Regiment to Nicaragua in 1912. Since 1917, Navy chaplains have served faithfully and loyally with the Marines from Belleau Wood to Desert Storm. And, of course, they have provided spiritual support for Marines and their families in peacetime as well.

Military chaplains are not a mere appendage to the Armed Forces. From the very beginning they have been an invaluable aid in the practical as well as spiritual needs of military personnel. They have not held themselves aloof from the suffering created by war, but have placed themselves right on the front lines with the men and women they serve. Within the darkness of war, they exist as beacons of light, representing man's nobler qualities and inviting him towards peaceful resolution to conflict. Father Vincent would enter this unique brotherhood of heroes and enrich its history by his own dedication to service and valor under fire.

Father Vincent's first step on the way to a commission was to make contact with the United States Navy Reserve in Hawaii. He arrived in Honolulu on August 23, 1965, and although he spent his first few weeks helping out at local Maryknoll parishes, he wasted no time beginning the necessary paperwork. Bishop Comber sent a formal letter as Superior General of Maryknoll to the office of the Military Ordinariate temporarily releasing Father Vincent to the military. This placed Father Vincent under the direct authority of Francis Cardinal Spellman, who seven years earlier had ordained him. Within a few years, Cardinal Spellman would also attend Father Vincent's funeral, one of his last public appearances before his own death a few months later.

Background checks and administrative procedures meant that Father Vincent would have to wait several months for his commission. He did not, however, live as a man holding his breath; rather, he embraced the sacrament of the present moment and gave himself totally to the missions in Hawaii. For three months he relieved Maryknoll Father Joseph Matheis, the pastor of a small Catholic church in Kamuela, a rural town in Western Hawaii. He also served the smaller mission parish of Puako on the western shore located just off the Queen Kaahumanu Highway.

Father Vincent spent only a short time at Annunciation Catholic Church in Kamuela, but even three decades later parishioners cherish his memory. He won their hearts with his warmth, his quiet smile, and his ever-present priestly character. His magnetic personality not only attracted people to him, but also made him quite memorable. Today, a picture of Father Vincent in his dress blue Navy uniform hangs in the vestibule of the church.

Leon Thevenin, one of Annunciation's sixty parishioners, remembered Father Vincent as "a prince of a person — very refined, quiet and extremely patriotic." Another parishioner, James Thomas, described Father Vincent as a real community man: "The first time you met him you automatically felt you knew him — he was well liked by all who knew him."

Thomas owned a steak house in Waimea, just outside of Kamuela, where Father Vincent would often have lunch. Over many meals, they talked about his imminent departure for Vietnam. Thomas had served with the Marines in Korea and knew combat well. He tried to talk Father Vincent out of volunteering for Vietnam, but the eager priest insisted that Vietnam was where he belonged and that he wanted to help the Marines. Thomas saw Father Vincent as a dedicated man of God who would serve the Marines well; but no one, especially a Marine who had experienced combat, could see the priest leave for Vietnam without serious concern.

In late November 1965, after waiting three months, Father Vincent finally received a letter confirming his appointment to the Chaplain Corps and ordering him to report for active duty on January 3, 1966, at the Naval Chaplains School in Newport, Rhode Island. His official date of rank is November 4, 1965. He accepted his appointment as a Lieutenant in the Chaplain Corps and was sworn in on December 28, 1965. Enthused about his new challenge, he changed the name on his pocket calendar for 1966 from "Rev." to "Lieutenant" Vincent Capodanno.

Our understanding of Father Vincent would be greater if we knew more about what he was thinking as he made this important change in his life. His eagerness to accept this new assignment was evident to everyone as he went about his work in Hawaii; but, for all his friendliness and self-sacrifice, he remained essentially a private person. Did he perhaps marvel at the turn his life had taken? After all, here was a man who had made a commitment to be a missionary — now embarking on a journey that would take him directly and willingly into war. Did he think back to the seminary in Ossining and its close proximity to the great military academy at West Point, smiling quietly at the realization of how far he had traveled, only to come to a career that was essentially "right down the road"?

The long flights to the mainland and across the North American continent surely provided an opportunity for reflection. Even so, one thing is certain: from the moment he had sent the cable-gram to Bishop Comber announcing his desire to be a military chaplain, Father Vincent was a man with a mission and he proceeded steadily and without hesitation towards his goal.

Chaplain Vincent Capodanno reported for his first duty assignment at the Chaplains School in Newport, Rhode Island (Class 1-66), on January 2, 1966. The Newport Naval Base is headquarters for many Navy schools, including the Officer Candidate School, Naval Academy Preparatory School, Naval War College and Chaplains School. All newly commissioned Navy chaplains must first go through a basic eight-week course in which they learn how to salute, identify rank, wear their uniforms and absorb an endless list of Navy regulations.

Chaplain Capodanno's class consisted of clergymen from all denominations, including Jews, Methodists, Episcopalians, Lutherans and Baptists. Upon graduation, the chaplains would be sent to different assignments — some to ships, others to bases. Each chaplain would have to be ready to minister to all personnel, regardless of their official religious affiliation. The ecumenical nature of military chaplaincy, which is lived out in the concrete situations of military life, is quite remarkable. The common denominator is that all men and women are children of their Heavenly Father, called to live a life in communion with God and each other. The military recognizes this spiritual dimension to man and provides for it with the same seriousness that it provides for physical needs.

Chaplain Victor Krulak, an Episcopal minister and one of Father Vincent's closest friends in Vietnam, noted that "few chaplains went from Chaplain School to Vietnam without prior military experience." To Chaplain Krulak's knowledge only he and his friend Vince were sent directly to Vietnam without such a background. Both had earnestly requested and eagerly sought to be assigned to the Marines in Vietnam. Perhaps, in Father Vincent's case, his knowledge of oriental traditions as well as his Asian missionary experience made his request quite reasonable to those responsible for his duty assignment. For Chaplain Krulak's part, his father, Lieutenant General Victor H. Krulak, USMC, commanded all Marines in the Pacific during Father Vincent's time in Vietnam.

The basic course in Rhode Island finished on February 24, 1966. Before leaving for his next training program at Camp Pendleton, California, Father Vincent spent a few weeks on leave at his sister Pauline's house. Once again, the Capodanno family surrounded their brother with a warm welcome and many parties. He celebrated daily Mass at Queen of Peace Catholic Church in North Arlington, New Jersey, about a mile from Pauline's home, becoming good friends with the priests there.

Father Vincent's time at home was all too short for the members of his family, but he was eager to get on with his duties. Those present for his departure couldn't help but remember the same scene eight years earlier when Rachel Capodanno said goodbye to the son she would not see again on this earth. At that time, the family bid farewell to a young missionary dressed in black priestly robes, bound for fields afar in Taiwan. Now, he stood before them, Lieutenant Vincent Capodanno, in the dress blue uniform of the United States Navy, on his way to serve with the Marines. If there had been some trepidation in sending him off to Taiwan eight years ago, the family was certain there was more to fear in the fields of Vietnam.

On March 16, 1966, Father Vincent reported for three weeks of training in the Field Medical Service School at Camp Pendleton, California. The school trained those assigned to Vietnam in battle first aid, counter-insurgency tactics, physical fitness, and survival skills. Although the subjects covered in the program were serious, Father Vincent seemed to enjoy himself. Always one to see the humor in a situation, he wrote to his brother:

> About half the group had never had any military service before and in the beginning, the drill classes looked something like the Marx Brothers running around. The DI [Drill Instructor] was a long, lean, well-seasoned Marine but even he nearly doubled up with laughter one morning.

During his short time at the school, Father Vincent met Lieutenant Paul Hubble, USMC, who was also training for his departure to Vietnam as a platoon leader. They both lived at the Camp Pendleton Bachelor Officers' Quarters, and after their days of training would often spend their nights talking. Lieutenant Hubble remembered Father Vincent fondly and recalled how easy it was to speak with him. They would often discuss the nature of the Asian people, especially those with whom the priest had worked in Taiwan. Hubble remembered Father Vincent's sense of humor when describing his experiences in Taiwan. One night he said to him:

> Did you know that the people's ancestors who I worked with in Taiwan were cannibals? They had given it up for some time but late at night around a fire after a bit of drinking the men would start bragging. 'My grandfather had two heads.' 'My great grandfather had four heads!' a different native claimed.

Father Vincent also developed a very close relationship with Chaplain Stanley Beach at the training school. Chaplain Beach was a Baptist minister and a former Navy enlisted man before entering the ministry. Beach rented a car so that the two of them could do some traveling during their short stay.

Father Vincent's spiritual manner and dedication to his vocation greatly impressed Beach: "[He] had an obvious sense of mission about life, he knew who he was, he knew why he was, and what he was about. I was a neophyte drawing on Vin's incredible formation and insights." He found Father Vincent to be a very determined man, yet his determination was tempered with wisdom and compassion. His resolve was to go to Vietnam. "Vince went into the Chaplain Corps with one thing in mind: to go to Vietnam," he remembered. "That was a consuming passion in everything he did."

Both talked about the "what ifs" of combat. Chaplain Beach remarked, "We had no illusions about what we would be facing, we knew we wanted to be with the troops, because that's what ministry is." Even years later, he recalled that when Father Vincent talked of being with the Marines, "His eyes would light up."

According to Beach, Father Vincent's way of doing ministry involved a lot of listening. "He would walk up, strike a conversation, ask ten questions, and you were pouring out your life before you knew it." Perhaps years of struggling with the Hakka dialect had refined Father Vincent's already quiet nature into one of careful attention. He would be remembered by the Marines for this ability to be fully present and with them in their conversations.

At last, paperwork and training behind him, Father Vincent reached his goal. During Holy Week of April 1966 he stepped onto the soil of Vietnam.

He would not have realized it at the time, but his arrival was congruent with the zenith of United States involvement in the war. The previous year, in March 1965, at the same time Father Vincent was requesting permission to serve as a military chaplain, President Johnson had ordered a major escalation of United States forces in Vietnam. By the end of 1965, 184,300 United States servicemen were in Vietnam and, just one year later, the troop commitment had more than doubled, reaching 385,300. Americans were suddenly taking more notice of affairs in Southeast Asia as casualties mounted dramatically. In the first quarter of 1965, seventy-one Americans were killed in Vietnam; in the last quarter, 920; and by 1966, an average of 400 U.S. soldiers per month were losing their lives.

Disapproval of the build-up was strong right from the beginning, but politicians and military advisors, together with a largely sympathetic media, continued to maintain that the situation was progressing in favor of South Vietnamese liberation. In the period immediately following Father Vincent's arrival in Vietnam, anti-war feeling in the United States would become more common, escalating finally into the violent protests of 1968. A beleaguered President Johnson was already attempting to defend his Vietnam policy in a speech given at John Hopkins University just five days before Father Vincent landed in Vietnam.

Father Vincent surely knew of the growing national tension over the conflict; but his agenda was not a political one. It is evident from his conversations with friends and family that he had no doubts about the justice of American military involvement in Southeast Asia. He had grown up during the World War II and believed in the triumph of freedom over tyranny; he had been formed in the Maryknoll tradition of heroic witness to the Gospel in the face of atheistic communism. His faith, his formation, and his own native goodness disposed him to aid a suffering and oppressed people. But even so, Father Vincent was not moved primarily by the larger political or even humanitarian picture; he looked rather to the young men fighting in Vietnam. He felt the need for a priestly presence among them, and he answered it with all his heart.

When Father Vincent arrived in Da Nang, Vietnam, he found two familiar companions waiting for him: the tropical climate, and the friendly face of Chaplain Beach who had arrived somewhat before him. The two men were temporarily placed in Da Nang until their regular assignments were made.

Da Nang was an important city at that time and it has left its mark on the annals of the history of the war. Lying on the east coast of South Vietnam bordering the China Sea, Da Nang was roughly equidistant between the then opposing Vietnamese capital cities: Saigon in the south and Hanoi in the north. Da Nang served as headquarters for the 3rd Marine Division and, resting within the Quang Nam Province, enclosed one of five provinces in the military area of operations known as "I Corps."

In a letter home, the missionary-turned-chaplain described the scene as he found it in Da Nang:

> I was semi-settled in my quarters within a few hours after arriving here. Quarters are tents and conditions of the field variety but well organized and more comfortable than really could be expected or hoped for under the conditions. Da Nang Enclave is only about six or seven months old. I am in a transient's tent until I receive a specific assignment. There are four engineers, three civilians and one Marine Major, sharing the tent but it is big enough for at least twelve people. They had one fan and I bought one in Okinawa so we are even cool. Food is good and plentiful and fans are now being installed in the mess-tent shared by the entire unit in this particular section.
>
> The Da Nang Enclave, or base of operations as it is sometimes called, surrounds on three sides the port-city (or town) of Da Nang. The local problems there do not touch upon the

base since the base is separated from the town and when there are difficulties, the town is closed to all Americans. It is now open but for official business only. I went in yesterday with one of the chaplains who had some things he wanted to bring to the Sacred Heart Orphanage. We went in (the orph. is in the heart of town next to the cathedral) visited with the kids and nuns for a few moments, left and returned with no difficulty . . . even got a big wave from one of the VN generals who was going into town in his staff car.

What Father Vincent fails to mention in this letter home was that he arrived in Da Nang during political unrest between civil Vietnamese political factions. The dissident activity was known as the "Struggle Movement," and caused the evacuation of all American civilians from the usually safe city of Da Nang. He never reported this type of news to his relatives; he was always positive and sometimes quite humorous.

Chaplain Beach remembered that his colleague was not at all happy waiting in Da Nang for an assignment. Chaplain Frank R. Morton, a Lutheran minister and a Navy Captain, was the Division Chaplain for the 3rd Marines and the detailer for arriving chaplains. Chaplain Morton took his time when it came to placing his men. Chaplains Capodanno and Beach stewed for two weeks anticipating word of their assignment to a Field Marine unit. During the "waiting game" they explored a little of the area and jumped at any chance to go to the "field" where the Marines were.

On Easter Sunday, just a few days after their arrival, the two chaplains enthusiastically accepted the opportunity to go to the front lines south of Da Nang — their first trip into a hostile area. Beach recalled the helicopters coming early Sunday morning to pick them up at "C" Med, a field hospital, and taking them to the troops returning from operation "Nevada." He recalled:

> We spent Easter Sunday morning ministering to those men. It made a deep impression on both of us and those moments of looking into the eyes of Marines who were experienced with death, gave us a greater appreciation of the hope of the Resurrection in Jesus Christ. Vin and I talked about that. He had tears in his eyes when he shared that experience.

It would have been no insignificant thing to Father Vincent to arrive in Vietnam during Holy Week. Every year of his life he had enjoyed the ritual splendor of this holiest of weeks when the Church celebrated her origin and her hope. Holy Week is traditionally a feast for the senses and the soul: beautiful vestments, the smell of incense, oil and flowers, traditional chants and hymns by seasoned choirs, packed churches and confessional lines — and following the religious ceremonies, family gatherings and feasting.

Holy Week in Vietnam was not so splendid, but it was just where Vincent Capodanno wanted to be. He did not want an easy, comfortable life. He looked for challenge — for the thing that would test his limits and make him go deeper. In Vietnam, he finally found the ultimate test. This year, what he had lived in mystery through signs and symbols, he now saw in the flesh: the true price of sin — death; and the object of Christian hope — eternal life. In this catechism of Vietnam, each of the days of Holy Week brought Vincent Capodanno to a new level of wisdom and compassion.

Holy Thursday is every priest's anniversary. During Christ's Last Supper with his beloved disciples, he left them two commandments. The first established the Eucharist, and thereby, the priesthood: "Do this in memory of me!" The second gave birth to the ministry of service, "Love one another as I have loved you." Together, these two commands formed one — to live as Christ Jesus lived, to be his on-going presence in the world. While every baptized Christian shares in this mission, priests are set apart in a particular way to make present the mysteries of Christ's life. In the consecration of the bread and wine, a priest speaks in the first person, "This is *my* body . . . *my* blood." These words remind him of the sacrifice of Christ and his own sacrifice. Saying these words now in Vietnam, looking into the eyes of each man as he distributed the Body of Christ in communion, Father Vincent felt a profound solidarity with these men who knew such incredible suffering. With an acute spiritual instinct he understood that he would sanctify men more by suffering with them than he would by preaching.

Good Friday, the day Jesus died, is the only day of the year when Mass is not said. In its place is the reading of the Passion of the Lord — up to his burial — and the Veneration of the Cross. For the first time, Father Vincent would read the passion alone, but in the intimacy of his heart, in the solitude that only a priest can know, he understood that every gesture of care and compassion he extended to his men would be his daily veneration of the Cross.

The prayerful expectation of Holy Saturday finally gave way to Easter morning. Standing at the altar, looking into the faces of men who every day were facing the finality of death, Father Vincent proclaimed the audacious words, "He has Risen!" That day, he heard as if for the first time, the words of the *Victimae Paschalis,* the traditional Easter hymn: in mortal combat death and life had met, and life emerged the victor. Such an announcement requires a witness. Father Vincent would give that witness every day of his sixteen months in Vietnam.

During that same week, a Marine Corps film unit was making a documentary about chaplains in Vietnam. The film, *For Thou Art With Me*, shows Father Vincent saying Mass, riding in a helicopter, and talking with a Marine about the war. One segment of the film reveals how he was able to get the Marines to talk about their problems by asking questions and listening. It reads:

Cap[odanno]: How are things out at the forts, then?

Marine: Well, pretty good, Father, except we lost another man last night.

Cap: Who, Benny?

Marine: Benny, yeah.

Cap: What happened to him?

Marine: Well we got our night ambush and (unclear) grenaded us. He caught a little shrapnel in the stomach.

Cap: How, how is he now?

Marine: They heli medevaced him that night. He's at First Med somewhere. Haven't seen him since.

Cap: Oh! I'm going out there. . . .

Lieutenant Colonel Carl K. Mahakian was in charge of the film project and recalled filming Father Vincent in one scene puffing on a cigarette. When the film was presented for review, someone in the Chief of Chaplains Office wanted to cut the "smoking scene," but Mahakian insisted it remain because it was real. A typical American fighting man of the sixties, Capodanno did enjoy smoking; in fact, he was known to be a chain smoker. He even learned how to smoke at night during battle. Lieutenant Frederick Smith taught him how to make a "smoking machine": you put a hole in a c-ration box and put the cigarette in the box under a poncho, thus being able to smoke without giving off a glow which could attract enemy fire.

Father Vincent Capodanno was not in Vietnam to make movies. He grew impatient waiting for his own place among his fellow marines and, after two weeks, demanded that Chaplain Morton give him an assignment. Beach recalled that after that meeting, things developed quickly. Chaplain Beach was sent to Happy Valley, a Marine base near Phu Bai, north of Da Nang, and Chaplain Capodanno was sent to the 7th Marine Regiment, south of Da Nang.

THE 7th MARINES

The apostle must be as much a man as possible.
Our Lord was a man in the fullest and most magnifi-
cent sense of the word. . . Responsive to all His breth-
ren, He is with them in their sorrows and their joys. . .
He is not pontifical or sententious, always He shows
Himself cordial, simple, approachable. His chief qual-
ity is His good-nature, 'a smiling self-abandonment.'

Raol Plus, S.J.,
Radiating Christ: An Appeal to Militant Catholics

The regimental headquarters for the 7th Marines was positioned close to an area called Chu Lai, about fifty miles directly
south of Da Nang, off National Route One, the main north-south
highway in coastal Vietnam. The South China Sea was only
about a mile and a half from the east side of the camp, and the
Chu Lai airfield was a mile to the north. The terrain of the area is
much like the sandy rolling dunes of the coastal Carolinas.

Under operational control of the 1st Marine Division head-
quartered in Da Nang, the regiment had approximately 3,500 to
4,000 Marines, who were organized into three battalions in a
crescent shape around the Chu Lai airfield. The battalions are
commonly referred to as 1/7, 2/7, and 3/7, with the battalion
number first and the regiment number last. Each battalion was
divided into four alphabetical companies; thus, 1/7 had companies A, B, C, D; 2/7 had E, F, G, H; and 3/7 had I, K, L, M.

On April 30, Father Vincent arrived by helicopter and reported for duty with the 7th Marines. He was assigned to 1st Battalion, 7th Marines, that was located on a peninsula south of Chu

Lai bordering on the Tra Bong River. At the 1st Battalion, he replaced Chaplain Robert J. Usenza, a lieutenant and a Catholic priest. While Father Vincent was specifically assigned to the 1st Battalion, he had to serve all the battalions in the 7th Marines because he was the only Catholic chaplain in the regiment. His ministry covered a wide area, requiring him to be constantly on the move, rarely with one battalion or company for more than a few days at a time.

When the chaplain was in his "home" battalion, he stayed in a tent, known as a "hootch." During a move across the river, however, Father Vincent was without a tent for some time. Major Edward Fitzgerald, who became a close friend, invited Vince to bunk with him and Lieutenant Jerry G. Pendas, operations officer of 1/7. Pendas did not like the idea of a chaplain bunking with Marines. To test Capodanno, he tacked up nude pictures all around the priest's cot. Father Vincent never said a word. After a few days, Pendas became embarrassed about the pictures and took them down.

As the story indicates, Father Vincent's ministry to the Marines was not one of words as much as presence. He was not standing on any soapboxes. The only thing he asked of the grunt Marines was the honor to be with them, and that meant he had to become one of them.

"Grunt Marine" is a term that by rights should only be used by enlisted infantry Marines. They use it to remind themselves of the seriousness of their training: sweat in peace saves lives in war.

Most of the Grunt Marines in Vietnam were young, usually eighteen or nineteen years old, and just out of high school. While some were there simply in accord with the draft, most felt a certain patriotic obligation to serve their country and fight for the cause of freedom for the Vietnamese people. They were a generation that had grown up with stories from World War II, told by their fathers, uncles and older friends. They believed they were following an honorable tradition and were willing to lay down their lives for it.

But this was not the same kind of war that their father's had fought. Vietnam was a small unit war, a war of raids, counter-raids, mines and booby traps. The distinction between enemy and civilian was unclear, as many a good-natured American was too late to discover. Futility became the watchword as Grunts saw their buddies shot down for a patch of land that would almost immediately be re-taken by the enemy. During their thirteen-month tour of duty Grunt Marines were fatigued from hours of boredom broken only by moments of terror.

Like all chaplains, Father Vincent was sent to these men to be their pastor, their father, and their friend. He was to help them cope with death and suffering, loneliness and depression, as well as the host of moral questions that good men reflect on during times of war. He was also there to give assistance to the medical corps: to help with the wounded and comfort the dying.

What set Father Vincent apart was the way he lived his ministry with the Marines. He was not a religious leader who did his job and then returned to the comfort of his own circle. He lived as a Grunt Marine. Wherever they went, he went. Whatever burdens they had to carry, he shared the load. No problem was too large or too small to take to Father Vincent — he was available to them day and night. In a short time, the Grunt Marines recognized Father Vincent's determination to be with them and one of them. They respectfully and affectionately dubbed him, "The Grunt Padre."

Lieutenant Commander Roy A. Baxter, a Southern Baptist Minister and the regimental chaplain for the Seventh, said of Father Vincent:

> He was accessible and he was approachable. The men felt comfortable around him and free to approach him for good conversation and with their needs. He lived day to day as they did, as a Marine. This identity enhanced the genuineness of his loving concern and care for their spiritual and other needs. He was one of them, he was truly their Padre.

During the sixteen months he served in Vietnam, Father Vincent was the best known and sought after chaplain in the Marine Corps, and a living hero. This claim is supported by accounts of his personal involvement in the lives of his Marines, his heroic acts during many battles, and the lasting impression he made as a man of peace and good humor.

"He attracted people," recalled Colonel Gerald H. Turley, then a major and the Seventh Regiment's logistics officer. "And yet, in that group, he would be the humblest guy there. I think that he felt that the young men had far bigger problems than he did and he did everything to bring comfort and joy to them."[1]

Major Ed Fitzgerald recalled an occasion when Father Vincent was able to help an extremely tall, black Marine whose feet were too large to fit into standard Marine boots. The Marine was restricted to base camp, walking in sandals, while his unit was actively engaged in the field. He longed to be with his comrades. He became depressed and felt he was letting his unit down. Father Vincent stepped in and personally solved the difficulty. He sent the Marine on R & R (rest and recreation leave) to Hong Kong where a pair of boots was tailor-made for him. When the Marine returned, he was able to participate with his unit and, as Major Fitzgerald said, "He became one of the finest young men I have ever met."

Major Fitzgerald also noted that Father Vincent spent most of his few spare hours writing letters of condolence and information to parents of wounded and dead Marines. The chaplain's pocket calendar, which he carried with him at all times, was filled with the names and addresses of these families. After Father Vincent himself became a casualty of the war, many of those who had received these letters wrote to the Capodanno family telling them what a consolation his letters had been. Mrs. Hobart Byrne wrote:

> Father Capodanno attended my son when he was wounded last April in Viet Nam. He wrote to us the same day Joe was wounded and assured us that he was in good condition. It had been a terrible week of worry for us, and his letter was the most important thing in the world to us. Father Capodanno wrote us again this summer asking about Joe, saying he had lost track of him. . . . I'm sure he took the same personal interest in many more Marines.

---

[1] Colonel Turley has written *The Easter Offensive*, a first hand account of the largest offensive action by North Vietnam.

A similar letter of gratitude was written by Mr. and Mrs. Ralph W. Dieterle:

> Although he had little time for himself, he took time out to write to the parents of a young boy he had administered the Last Rites to in Viet Nam last year, Lieutenant Corporal Thomas Tamiliao, our nephew. We only wish we could write and give you the consolation he wrote and gave to Tom's parents and all of us who needed it at that time.

Mrs. Herrington also wrote about Father Vincent's personal care:

> He was Chaplain of our late son Lieutenant Corporal Raymond N. Herrington's unit in 1966. On Dec. 9th/66 Father was sent as Chaplain to a hospital. On Dec. 10th our son was wounded and taken to that hospital. Father was with him almost every hour of the two days our son was there before being sent to Clark Air Base. Father helped our son write us a letter (his last) telling us of his wounds. We were so thankful someone who knew our Ray quite well was with him his last few days of life on this earth. . . . Father wrote us several letters after our son's death which will always be a treasure to us.

Father Vincent also spent time writing letters to organizations that could help supply the Marines with gifts. He wrote the following request during the Christmas season of 1966:

> If you are wondering if it is possible to send a package for our men here at Christmas time: it is. If you would like, you can send something to me and I will pass it on to the Marines. I would suggest such things as: canned candy; canned food not usually found in Mess halls; goodies of various kinds; smoking pipes; paper-back books; some sort of compact writing-portfolio; water proof plastic zippered bags for keeping papers, documents etc; pen sized flashlights with a good supply of batteries and bulbs; cigarette lighters and flints; sweat-shirts with a lot of color or some humorous design.

The following spring, Father Vincent wrote again thanking those who sent gifts:

> It was really wonderful to hear from everyone at Christmas time and your response to my request for packages and

mail was indeed overwhelming. Our men here enjoyed immensely all the goodies you sent and were most pleased and happy that so many people thought of them during the Holidays. The packages, the cards, notes, and letters really gave everyone's morale a boost. It was most kind of you all and I, as well as all the men, thank you for your generosity.

Father Vincent assisted the regiment in many other ways. Captain Richard "Dick" Alger, intelligence officer (also known as the S-2) for the 7th Marine Regiment, remembered his help in the evacuation of the civilians of a small hamlet near Chu Lai. The people of the hamlet were worried about the threat of the Communist takeover, so the villagers asked to be moved closer to the military camp. The evacuation had to take place on foot because helicopters and vehicles would arouse suspicion. Everything — pigs, furniture, and farming equipment — had to be carried out. Father Vincent helped in the evacuation by carrying out supplies in the rain and mud right alongside the Marines.

Sergeant Charles Carmin, Senior NCO of D Company 1/7, remembered Father Vincent as a true mud Marine who was always in the field with the enlisted men. He was particularly grateful for the chaplain's presence after the painful death of one of his Marines. A routine and "safe" operation had unexpectedly turned into a nightmare. In the bloody ambush, an eighteen-year-old radio operator was shot in the kidney — a critical wound. Carmin picked up the wounded man and drove him frantically back to the battalion first aid station. The young Marine kept pleading with Carmin not to let him die. Father Vincent was at the aid station when Carmin arrived. He personally responded to the emergency and flew with the wounded Marine to the field hospital; but during the short helicopter flight, the young man died. Father Vincent returned to the battalion and helped the living, especially Sergeant Carmin, deal with the loss and the guilt. This story of comfort and compassion in the face of death is retold countless times by the Marines who served with Father Vincent.

In addition to being present with the Marines in their emotional and physical suffering, as well as the "roll up your sleeves" kind of ministry that placed him right alongside them during their special assignments, there were also occasions for formal religious training. Sergeant Grady Studdard, who was preparing to enter the Catholic Church at that time, received over seventy-five hours of catechetical instruction from Father Vincent. Studdard detailed his chaplain's teaching method:

> He covered the Old Testament almost in its entirety; all but the last chapter of St. Matthew; a survey history of the Church with emphasis on the Protestant reformation. I still have the Bible he presented me, after completion of the instructions. It has been 24 years since that hot miserable summer, but one does not forget men like Father Cap. Having traveled in the Holy Land, he could truly tell a story that would literally keep me waiting for the next session.

In late July 1966, the 1st Battalion moved across the Tra Bong River south of Chu Lai airfield. During the move, Battalion Commander, Lieutenant Colonel Frederick S. Wood gave Father Vincent permission to pick the site for a new chapel and to supervise its construction, using native materials. Father Vincent wrote:

> We are going to be moving across the river sometime soon. The new area is being worked on and the sites for the various buildings have already been assigned...the Colonel gave the choicest site to the chapel. We are going to have a new chapel of bamboo and thatch built beginning early next week [end of July]. It will be the same size as the present one, sixteen ft wide and forty-eight long but will be much better since it will be new.

Major Ed Fitzgerald, the executive officer of the battalion, remembered that the money used to build the new chapel was collected at a beer party for the whole battalion. Father Vincent briefly referred to the chapel in a letter home:

> I am attached to the 1st of the three battalions of the 7th Regiment (also called 7th Marines) located now in the Chu Lai area of Viet Nam. Our Battalion Headquarters are on the hills running along the banks of a picturesque river. It is here that I live and here that we have a bamboo and coconut-thatch chapel. Incidentally, coconut tree branches form a more waterproof thatch than does straw . . . just in case you are ever required to make the choice!

Father Vincent took great pride in this chapel because he wanted to show the Marines that their faith was important and they deserved to have a proper place to worship. The chapel could accommodate a little more than 100 people and was usually full to overflowing during services.

Two newspaper articles written about Father Vincent while he served with the 7th Marines give us a rare glimpse of him in the field with his grunts. It is remarkable how this Catholic priest became so beloved of the Marines in such little time; further, these articles show us what must have been the sorrow and loss felt by all of his grunts when their chaplain became a casualty of war.

The first article, by Kenneth Armstrong, is called "Padre Is the 7th Regiment Marines' Morale Booster on Cong Hunt." It appeared in the *Cleveland Plain Dealer* and elsewhere on September 4, 1966, exactly one year before Father Vincent was killed. Here is the article in its entirety:

NAM TRAM PENINSULA, South Viet Nam—Up and down the marine column, I heard the whispered words, 'The padre's coming with us!'

And the reaction 'Number 1!'

The padre, the armed forces term for a chaplain, whether Protestant, Catholic or Jewish, was a tanned and fit Maryknoll Father, Navy Lieutenant Vincent Capodanno of Staten Island, N.Y.

Superficially, he could not be distinguished from other officers. He did not wear insignia of rank. That is standard in the field—the Viet Cong concentrates its fire at officers—but everybody in Alpha Company, 1st Battalion 7th Regiment Marines, knew who he was.

As we hiked with the Marines that sweltering day, we had a chance to talk during the occasional rest breaks. Like the Marines, he had a crewcut under his helmet but unlike the young Leathernecks, his hair was stained with gray, a hint of his age, 37.

He wore a flak jacket, normal equipment for the Marines, and I kidded him 'Father, that's not a very good advertisement for your faith—that flak jacket!'

Laughing, he replied: 'I know it, but it's protective coloration so I blend in with the men. In addition, I understand their trials better if I accept the same burdens they do, such as wearing the jacket and carrying a pack.'

A onetime missionary in Taiwan and Hong Kong, Fr. Capodanno volunteered for service in January, and after five weeks of physical conditioning at Camp Pendleton, Calif., was assigned Catholic chaplain for the 7ᵗʰ Marine Regiment at Chu Lai. His schedule is hectic.

'My tent is at 7ᵗʰ Battalion headquarters, and I conduct mass there each morning. But during the day, I circulate among all the battalions,' he said.

'Sunday is my busiest day, of course, and I serve at least three masses—at regimental headquarters and two or more at battalions. In a week, I hold a minimum of 15 masses.'

'How often do you go on operations?' I asked.

'I make all battalion-size operations,' he replied, 'and as many company-size as possible.'

'Why?'

'Well, I want to be available in the event anything serious occurs; to learn firsthand the problems of the men, and to give them moral support, to comfort them with my presence.

'In addition, I feel I must personally witness how they react under fire—and experience it myself—to understand the fear that they feel.'

'Have you been ambushed yet?' I asked.

'No, he answered seriously, just general fire. And believe me, I was frightened! You have no idea where it's coming from or who it's aimed at. And like everybody else. I dread the possibility of stepping on a booby trap.'

'What is the general attitude toward religion of these young Marines?'

'Very healthy,' he answered, 'by both Catholics and Protestants.'

'Sometimes, that's hard to believe,' I countered, 'in view of the language I often hear!'

Chuckling, he commented: 'I know what you mean. I thought I knew all of the bad words, but I've learned a few new ones over here! However, their swearing is frequently a release. They don't realize what they're saying.'

'Do many of them come to you with problems?'

'They certainly do. I spend much of my time counseling, discussing their problems with them.'

'What kind of problems?' I inquired.

'The usual ones. Mainly, problems at home with their family, a wife or a girlfriend. Surprisingly, the biggest problem is when a boy doesn't get any mail from home.'

'Do they ever discuss the moral issue of killing?'

'No, I don't think anyone has ever raised it. To them, this is a job—a nasty job—and that's part of it. Prior to a big operation, some will come to me, but primarily to reinforce their faith.'

'What about our involvement in Viet Nam?' I asked. 'Do they question it?'

'No, they accept it as a necessary evil of the world today,' he replied. 'And their courage! It's unbelievable. Whether it's going into combat, on patrol, or entering a Viet Cong cave not knowing what's below!'

During the long sweep through the wilting heat, Fr. Capodanno never faltered. It was apparent that the Marines were pleased with his presence.

Near the end of the long day, a few approached and shyly said, 'Padre, thanks for coming. It meant a lot to us to have you along.'

He answered with a grin, 'In a way, it was very selfish of me, because I really enjoyed being with you.' And he meant it.

The other article, "Chaplain, Ex-Taiwan Missionary Feels His Job Is With Viet Troops," was written by the Marine Corps Press. The piece appeared in *The American Weekend* on October 19, 1966.

CHU LAI, Vietnam, Sept. 18—He moved quietly from one wounded Marine to another speaking softly to each man.

Wearing no weapon, his hands were stained with blood where he had rested a comforting palm on a critically wounded Marine's head.

Over one Marine he said the last rites and then sat back exhausted watching the helicopters medically evacuate the last of the wounded.

A splotch of blood was caked on his forehead where he had wiped sweat from his brow during the aftermath of a Viet Cong booby trap explosion.

Chaplain Vincent R. Capodanno, 37, of New York City, wears no physical weapon of war.

His only armament is faith—a basic, necessary and treasured attribute to the men around him. He is one of 20 Navy Chaplains serving in the 1ˢᵗ Marine Division and one of 63 in the III Marine Amphibious Force.

When the 1ˢᵗ Bn., Seventh Marine Regiment goes to the field, Chaplain Capodanno goes with them. He is their chaplain.

He moves among the men, changing companies from day to day so he can be with each unit for some time during an operation.

As a naval officer he is new to service life, but not to the primitive situation that Vietnam lends.

Before joining the Navy Chaplain's Corps in December 1965, Lieutenant Capodanno served six and a half years as a missionary in Taiwan, Nationalist China.

He worked with the natives, high in Taiwan's mountainous regions.

'This kind of life isn't new to me,' the Chaplain said during a recent operation. 'In Taiwan our missionary program was somewhat like the civil affairs program in Vietnam. We moved from village to village, living quite basic most of the time.'

Father Capodanno speaks one dialect of Chinese. He belongs to the Catholic Foreign Missionary Society and is a Maryknoll Father dedicated to spreading the faith in the Far East.

'My job here in the field with the men is kind of a morale booster. I'm around if they want to talk and I try to speak with as many of them as possible,' he said.

'I joined the Chaplain Corps when the Vietnam war broke out because I think I'm needed here as are many more chaplains. I'm glad to help in the way I can.'

As he moves among the men of the 1ˢᵗ Battalion, the talk is not always of religion. There is simple talk of men's hopes and aspirations, of men's strength's and weaknesses—all weighed and carefully surmised by the combat assigned chaplain.

There always seems to be a place reserved beside a wounded Marine—a place reserved for Father Capodanno who always seems to appear at the stricken Marine's side to speak or pray at the moment it is most needed.

Father Vincent developed close relationships with many of the chaplains, officers and grunts of the 7th Marines. Their personal impressions of Father Vincent paint a very powerful portrait of the kind of man into which he was evolving as he went about his ministry with the Grunt Marines.

"He was an outstanding chaplain!" asserted Chaplain David J. Casazza, Captain, Catholic priest and First Marine Division Chaplain. Casazza was responsible for all the Navy chaplains assigned to the Corps in Vietnam. As his superior, he perceived Chaplain Capodanno to be a very quiet person who knew what he wanted — and what he wanted more than anything was to be in the field with the Marines. He truly loved the Marines and wanted to spend the rest of his career serving with the Corps. This point is clearly seen by the fact that, when Father Vincent filled out the "next duty preference" form, also known in military circles as a "career wish list," he specified nine billet selections, all of which were with the Marine Corps.

The nearest priest to Father Vincent was Chaplain Richard Hunkins, a lieutenant and chaplain for the Seabees, who operated in the Chu Lai area. They went to confession to one another and, if at all possible, met on Sunday nights for dinner. Hunkins recalled that Father Vincent was a serious business-like guy but always fun to be around.

Chaplain Hunkins also noted that Father Vincent loved the Orient and came to have a special feeling for the Vietnamese, a fact attested to by his involvement in the Marines' social programs. The Marine Corps supported a Combined Action Program (CAP) in which small Marine units in conjunction with South Vietnamese Popular Forces protected and sustained local villages in the Chu Lai area from the threat of communism. Father Vincent was very interested in this project. He made many visits and became a valued asset to the villagers of Binh Yen Noi and the Marines at Fort Page in the village. He often helped to settle differences of opinion between the Marines of Company C, 1/7 who were assigned to the CAP and the villagers of the Binh Nghia area. His positive actions were mentioned in the book *The Village* by F. J. West, Jr., which documents the history of the program.

Unfortunately, a part of the Vietnam War was the civilian massacres at My Lai and My Khe in March 1968. The American media, growing distrustful of the military, saw these travesties as evidence of official and brutal misconduct. And, yet, there were many, many American servicemen who cared deeply about the Vietnamese and did much to help them. Father Vincent was one of these.

No doubt his appreciation for the Vietnamese people was partly the result of his work in Taiwan. He became, in fact, an expert on Asia. He often gave lectures to fellow chaplains and officers on the proper understanding of oriental culture. One such lecture, entitled "Some Reflections On Adaptation to the Orient," emphasized that the Vietnamese should not be treated like children who could not survive without our help, but as people who wanted assistance to better themselves.

Chaplain J. D. Shannon, a lieutenant and Presbyterian minister, remembered Father Vincent from the Chaplains School in Newport and from seeing him occasionally in Vietnam. Shannon commented on the priest's great love for all people, including the Vietnamese, and his philosophy behind serving them. Four months after Father Vincent's death, Shannon wrote Pauline Costa on this subject:

> From time to time I saw Vince in his work at the hospital. I remember one day we were having a cup of coffee together and were discussing the "people-to-people" (Civic Action) program. Vince loved the Vietnamese people. In fact he loved *all* people. But he had very definite opinions about how Americans should deal with the Vietnamese. Vince wanted to be certain they were shown respect and honor, and that the Vietnamese would not simply be prize winners in a hastily-rigged U.S. give away program. Vince has much valuable insight. He understood people, particularly Asian [sic] people.

Fortunately he made his thoughts and points clear to many persons, both officers and men. It is hard knowing how many positive values were realized because of Vince's concern, but I'm sure his influence was far-reaching.

As much as he loved and respected the Vietnamese people, Father Vincent never lost sight of his priorities. Major Ray J. Savage, communication officer for 1/7, recalled a specific occasion where he refused to lose his primary focus:

> As with many heroes, there was nothing spectacular or particularly striking about Chaplain Capodanno's personality aside from his total dedication to the Marines he served. He was, in fact, almost 'tunnel visioned' concerning his ministry to the Marines. I remember once, as the Battalion [sic] Civil Affairs Officer, asking him to assist me in something or other with the local Vietnamese (I believe it was to hold a mass in a nearby hamlet), to my astonishment and perplexity he refused me forthright. He explained to me that his ministry was to the Marines of his unit — not to the local population. To my knowledge he held to that philosophy.

While Father Vincent's large heart embraced all the children of God, he was first and foremost the servant of the ones to whom he had been sent. The Grunt Marines knew that they had first place in the heart of their chaplain, and they reciprocated his singleness of devotion with their own. It seems there was nothing his grunts would not do for him. On one occasion, Chaplain Hunkins' jeep was stuck in the mud and required a tank to tow it to the nearest camp, which just happened to be that of Father Vincent's battalion. Father Vincent took one look at the mud-caked jeep and asked a few of the grunts to clean it up for Hunkins. In thirty minutes the jeep looked as good as new

Sergeant Studdard, the Marine who received his religious instruction from Father Vincent, was one such grunt who made sure his chaplain always had what he needed. Sergeant Studdard explained:

> My duties were such, that would allow me to arrange for Father to have a jeep and driver plus an extra Marine guard, for when he traveled out of the Command Post to visit 'his Marines' in the field. He would refer to the Marines as his pa-

rishioners. He would always try and persuade me to let him drive so as not to endanger the lives of others, and that's the way he was. So unselfish and thoughtful of others. I would get ice for his personal use. He would give it away. He had a tent that also served as his office/sleeping quarters, which consisted of a cot and a field desk. Next to his cot I had ordered that a foxhole be dug, and sandbags surround his quarters, in case of mortar fire or enemy attacks he could merely roll into the hole. It was never used, when the bullets flew, he flew. I never told him that I knew he was giving his ice away. I just continued to furnish it. He did not just hold services on Sunday, he would be out in the field sharing the hardships and misery. His presence really did inspire the troops to feel better.

Lieutenant Pendas recounted two stories where "Padre," as he called Father Vincent, was concerned about the welfare of his Grunts:

A simple, but welcome shower was provided each night for the enlisted infantrymen in an open field with a few canvases set up to provide some privacy. They would walk to the shower area with only a towel, a bar of soap, and sandals. For some returning from the field, it had been weeks since their last shower. They would head directly to the spot, strip right there and get in, only to find themselves in a few minutes dripping wet with no towel. If Father Vincent happened to be using the shower at the same time, he would always give his towel to one of the helpless Marines and asked only that it be returned to his tent near the chapel. The chaplain would then have to walk back to his tent wearing nothing. When the young Marine returned the towel, Father Vincent would offer him a soda or beer, a book to read (he kept a well-stocked bookcase for this purpose) and, if needed, a place to bunk for the night. Often whole platoons arrived and Father would give hospitality to each Marine.

Pendas also recalled a typical day during monsoon season. Both he and Father Vincent needed to take a scheduled truck trip to regimental headquarters. The cab of the truck held only the driver and one other. Pendas insisted that the chaplain, being of higher rank, should sit in the cab while he got soaking wet in the open back of the truck. Two eighteen-year-old Grunts also needed a ride to headquarters. Without hesitation, Father Vincent convinced the two Grunts to squeeze into his seat in the cab. He then climbed into the back with Pendas who could not believe that he gave up his place so two Grunt Marines could stay dry and warm. The chaplain just smiled.

Colonel Turley recalled his first meeting with Father Vincent. On a typical hot and rainy night, Turley went to his tent for a few hours of rest. Upon entering, he noticed a Marine curled up under his tent flap trying to get some sleep while getting very wet from the rain. Turley thought the man was a young Marine who, because of darkness, couldn't get back to his unit. He went over to invite him to sleep in his tent and in the dim light saw that this was no Grunt but Father Vincent looking for a place to sleep after making a visit to one of the many companies of the regiment. The two men became fast friends. Father Vincent would stay overnight with Turley about twice a week as he rotated through the area. "He was a humble person," Turley recalled, "who obviously was at peace with himself in a place where war was going on."

Major Fitzgerald began his close relationship with Father Vincent through curiosity. Fitzgerald regularly walked by Father Vincent's tent at night and often noticed a light coming through the tent flap. He wondered if this chaplain ever slept and, to find out, he introduced himself. They spent many nights talking and grew to greatly appreciate each other's friendship.

On one occasion Father Vincent and Fitzgerald went on R&R together in Hong Kong. Father Vincent knew Hong Kong well and had many Maryknoll friends in the city. Fitzgerald remembered his boundless generosity and thoughtfulness while they vacationed there. The night before they returned to Vietnam, Fitzgerald noticed a gold necklace in a shop window that he wanted to send to his wife. The shop was closed, and there seemed to be no hope of buying the necklace. However, Father Vincent took the time to find out through a Maryknoll friend who owned the shop and had the store opened especially for Fitzgerald to purchase the necklace.

Father Vincent, true to his Italian roots, enjoyed a good meal. When he and Fitzgerald were out together, he would order the finest Scotch and wines, always insisting on paying the bill afterwards. Father Vincent displayed a great naturalness. He was at peace with himself and the world, and his love of life acted like a medicine on the men around him. Wherever he was, and whatever he had — everything was offered to ease and elevate the lives of others. Chaplain Roy Baxter commented on his extraordinary sense of hospitality:

> Vince was affable to all he met. It was always a pleasure to see him. I felt a genuine warmth of hospitality when I visited him at his tent. He always had time for you. I vividly see him now with a towel draped around his neck and down his chest, coping with the torrid and humid weather that was prevalent. It was an oasis of spiritual and social depth, a fraternal fellowship — a respite from my own duties. Though he had no refrigeration system, he would always have a can of soft drink to offer you. . . . [H]e put the welfare of others above his own.

During his tenure with the 7th, the most dramatic evidence of Father Vincent's love for his Marines was shown vividly and repeatedly in his acts of bravery on the battlefield. He participated in six combat operations while assigned to 1/7 in 1966. In chronological order, the operations were: "Montgomery," May 10–15; "Mobile," May 25–28; "Franklin," July 26–28; "Fresno," September 8–16; "Golden Fleece," September 17–27; and "Rio Blanco," November 20–27. The following testimonials recount Father Vincent's action under fire.

Major Savage commented on Father Vincent's determination to be assigned to the company with the greatest risk in the field.

> I recall that during staff briefings prior to an operation, Chaplain Capodanno always inquired of the intelligence officer which company would more likely be most exposed to enemy fire and subject to the highest casualties. That would be the one Chaplain Capodanno placed himself with.
>
> During any operation of more than two or three days duration, Chaplain Capodanno would manage to hop a ride, by whatever means available, to each company as well as the Battalion Command Group to talk with the men and officers and to minister in whatever way the situation called for. I think he had a great calming affect on all those with whom he came in

contact. The ministry of presence was no better demonstrated by any chaplain I have ever been associated with than Chaplain Capodanno.

Captain Raymond Leidich, Commanding Officer of A Company, 1/7, noted that Father Vincent always wanted to be with the troops on combat operations:

> He asked to go on patrol with my company whenever we were scheduled for company ops [operations]. As I recall, he went out with us three or four times in the ten weeks or so that I commanded the company. He was always interested in what the purpose of the patrol would be and knowing what was actually going on as the patrol proceeded. He was cool under fire and did not seem to be particularly concerned about his personal safety.
>
> I recall his compassion not only for my Marines and corpsmen but also for the Vietnamese citizens whose villages we visited. . . . He treated the villagers with compassion and comforted them on every opportunity.

Chaplain Baxter recalled Father Vincent's disregard for his own safety during operation "Montgomery," their first operation together.

> Vince's assignment during an operation was with the Battalion Aid Station where he ministered to the wounded and dying. . . . During the first night [of battle], the VC [Viet Cong] had come out of a well-concealed network of cunningly devised tunnels in strategic proximity to the Battalion CP (Command Post) bivouac and launched a grenade assault. Without regard for his own safety, Vince exposed himself while he held a flashlight for the corpsmen treating the casualties. . . . From the very outset, I was impressed that Vince possessed the desirable quality of poise — which was characteristically manifest throughout my tour with him.

In the fall of 1966, 1/7 was engaged in fierce combat operations during "Fresno" and "Golden Fleece." The battalion was assigned to the village of Van Ha, about forty miles south of Chu Lai. The mission of the battalion was to supervise the national elections, which the Viet Cong tried to disrupt, and to protect 7,000 tons of rice from falling into enemy hands. After the successful operations were completed and the Communists defeated, over 5,000 South Vietnamese citizens lined the streets to thank the Marines.

Father Vincent played an active and critical role in both operations. Major Alger recalled being with Father Vincent during the election day of 1966. From a hillside about two miles from the polling place, they were watching the Vietnamese vote with amazing perseverance despite the constant shelling from the Viet Cong. Father Vincent humorously commented that he thought Staten Island was a tough place to vote, and ardently noted that Americans back in the States had forgotten what a cherished thing freedom is and what it meant to fight for it.

The Commander of 1/7, Lieutenant Colonel Basile Lubka, officially noted in a fitness report how much the fighting Marines valued Father Vincent's devotion. He wrote:

> Chaplain Capodanno relentlessly provided the battalion with the solace, comfort, spiritual leadership and moral guidance so essential to an effective infantry battalion. He never spared himself. His dedication to duty will stand as a hallmark to Naval Chaplains everywhere. He exhibited those rare qualities of humanity, selflessness, and humility that are seldom achieved, even by Chaplains. He possessed those intangible qualities which all members of the battalion, officer and enlisted, regardless of religious affiliation, respected. He earned this respect not only as a chaplain, but as a unique human being. He had an uncommon understanding of people and an intimate knowledge of the social and religious customs of Vietnam.

> In truth, he was the "Padre." This was not a perfunctory title, but rather a reflection of the significant respect all hands had for him. This respect was earned by his total and complete willingness to share at all times the risks and privations of all members of the command. He suffered when the men suffered. He was their "Rock of Ages." Of his own volition, on operations, he deployed with the assault companies because he knew his services would be most needed by them. Within the TAOR [Tactical Area of Responsibility], he spent more days and nights at company combat bases than within the battalion CP. No problem was too small for him. All hands

sought actively his sage counsel. He did not proselytize; he served God, Corps, and mankind in an uncommon, courageous and inspiring way. His name will be legendary to those members who served with him in the 1st Battalion, 7th Marines. He was as vital to the operations of the battalion as is close air support and artillery. No Marine could know Chaplain Capodanno and not be an infinitely better human being for it.

The glowing remarks of Lieutenant Colonel Lubka were echoed by many of the Seventh, including the enlisted men. Sergeant William L. DeLoach stated:

Upon numerous occasions, I have seen Father go to wounded Marines, while the unit was under heavy fire, to offer religious and moral support. His constant presence was of great benefit to all Marines, young and old.

He was constantly seeking ways to make the trials of war a little more livable for the men. Father's many friends were constantly sending gifts to be distributed to the men of the Battalion.

During the monsoon seasons, Father continued to visit the companies of the battalion, even though the roads were almost impassable. The Father's visits were always a highlight in the Marines day, whether it be at the unit's combat base or in the field on combat operations.

On three separate occasions, when the odds were so great against the men of "C" Company, the friendly and consoling voice of Father gave added spirit and courage to the men. His courage in these situations was transplanted to the men of the unit.

In recommending Chaplain Capodanno for the Bronze Star, Major Fitzgerald also wrote an official account of his exemplary behavior on and behind the front lines:

Father Capodanno was particularly adept in putting men in the proper frame of mind before and during battle. He had the confidence and deep respect of the men and healed the scars which the loss of a friend frequently caused in those who survive. He eliminated bitterness from the hearts and instilled Christian determination and morals to be drawn against in future battles. He encouraged the men of all faiths to do more for their God, our Country, their Corps and themselves.

Few men have seen more combat action than their Chaplain. Invariably, he sought out that unit which was most likely to encounter the heaviest contact. He would then go with that unit and continually circulated along the route of march. During breaks, never resting, he moved among the men. His bravery, his humor, his right word at the right time contributed to the success of the unit.

He was particularly adept in observing a Marine who was troubled by the press of events and/or personal problems and who needed help and encouragement. He would share his rations and his cigarettes as he quietly shared his thoughts with these men. Troubles seemed to disappear. Men found themselves after these informal sessions with this chaplain.

While in the battalion combat base he worked long hours. He established a library, wrote hundreds of letters to parents, and counseled the troops. He was firm and fair. When convinced a Marine needed help he spared no energy and left no stone unturned in assisting him. But through his influence men accepted their responsibilities. He instilled proper attitudes in the minds of the men toward the Vietnamese, and toward each other.

He always worked long into the night after his late hour visitors had departed his office. During the day he visited the outlying company bases and hospitals to offer prayer and revisit those with whom he had walked into combat. Frequently he went on small unit patrols. More than one young NCO patterned himself upon the examples of leadership and bravery set by Chaplain Capodanno.

At Christmas he gathered gifts from friends and organizations all over the world to insure that no man in the Battalion was forgotten. He spent his own money to give his men items not readily available to them. On one occasion I witnessed Father Capodanno remove his rain suit and give it to a wounded Marine. For the remainder of the operation he was without suitable rain clothing.

Two other officers who witnessed Father Vincent's valiant action during Operation "Rio Blanco" contributed their accounts to the official record. Captain Kenneth W. Johnson observed his actions on November 22 in Phuong Dinh hamlet, where the 3rd

Platoon of M Company came under fire. Captain Johnson noted:

> In the ensuing firefight one Marine was wounded. Several Marines unknowingly stepped into a swollen stream, and two Marines were drowned and were lost in the swift current. Chaplain Capodanno immediately joined the search party which went to the scene of the firefight. During the several despairing hours before the bodies were recovered, he remained with the Third Platoon. By his presence he helped to inspire and sustain the successful search for the missing Marines.

On November 25, Captain David L. Walker was wounded in an open, flat rice paddy during Operation Rio Blanco. Walker, who lay helplessly in pain and exposed to enemy fire, needed aid if he was to survive. Walker stated:

> Father Capodanno was the first at my side, even though he had to run about 75 meters through heavy enemy small arms fire. After summoning a Corpsman he then assisted in carrying me to a safe area where I was med-evaced. During this time he was constantly exposed to enemy fire.

Father Vincent's aide, Corporal Henry Hernandez, also remembered the solace the chaplain provided to Captain Walker and others during Rio Blanco. He recalled:

> Father Capodanno was kneeling beside Captain Walker, exposed to enemy fire, whispering in his ear, as he did to all Marines that were wounded. He would say some words of comfort, that medical help was coming and say a prayer. Those that were killed in action, he would whisper the Act of Contrition in their ear. He told me that God would hear it and would forgive all their sins.

For his efforts during his six combat operations, Chaplain Vincent Capodanno received the Vietnamese Cross of Gallantry with Silver Star and the Navy Bronze Star. Both medals were awarded for exceptional meritorious service. The personal award of these prestigious honors by a chaplain is quite extraordinary.

Yet, Father Vincent's family were not even aware until after his death that he had participated in so much action or that he received any kind of citation. These were not things he would write about in his letters. He was not in Vietnam for medals and glory. He went to Vietnam expressly to be with the troops, to learn and to live the full meaning of Maryknoll Bishop Ford's motto, "to suffer with," and by doing so save souls and give glory to God. Even if Vietnam was a different kind of field afar, Father Vincent was still a Maryknoll missionary. The fact was that his ministry as a missionary priest had blossomed in Vietnam unlike anything he had been able to achieve in Taiwan. He was progressing along the path of holiness — a path of suffering, sacrifices, and a renunciation of many of life's pleasures, but also of true joy and Christian love. The Marines who knew Father Vincent in Vietnam remember him as a very happy and fulfilled priest.

The descent and incarnation described in *Radiating Christ* had brought Father Vincent now to suffering and burial. The more he united himself with his Grunts, the more he was united to Christ. As Christ suffered with and for those whom he loved, Father Vincent endured the trials of war with and for his Grunts. His own identity was receding; Christ's image was better able to radiate through him. The fastidious missionary of Taiwan had become a "mud Marine" and gloried in the designation. It would be too simple to say that Father Vincent was happy simply because he was being true to an ideal. The secret of his peace, of the happiness that he radiated to all, was the fulfillment he experienced in the intimate union he lived with God through and in those he loved — his Marines. This is a true burial: to rest in the heart of love.

PRIEST OF GOD — SERVANT OF MEN

We have to make Christian teaching attractive by presenting it in action, by furnishing an example of Christian life which will be not only attractive, but, if possible, even heroic. We have to make the truth admirable. Words may be effective; but actions have a hundred times their value in power of persuasion. And among actions the most persuasive of all are those which are marked with the stamp of heroism.

Raoul Plus, S.J.,
Radiating Christ: An Appeal to Militant Catholics

Normally, chaplains are transferred from field combat units after six months, but this was not the case with Father Vincent. After eight months of serving with the 7th, he was sent to a "rear" assignment. Chaplain Lawrence Lowry, a Roman Catholic priest, replaced Father Vincent at the 7th.

On December 8, 1966, Chaplain Casazza transferred Father Vincent to 1st Medical Battalion. Located only a short distance from 1st Battalion Headquarters in the area of Chu Lai, the 1st Medical Battalion served as one of four medical "field hospitals" for Marine and civilian casualties. All the medical personnel, from the doctors and nurses to the X-ray technicians and corpsmen, were Navy officers and enlisted men and women. The Marine Corps relied on the Navy not only for chaplains, but also for medical staff.

The goal of these field hospitals was to stabilize the wounded Marine for transport to the hospital ships *Repose* or *Sanctuary* in the South China Sea, or to other Naval hospitals in Hawaii,

Guam, Japan or the continental United States. The wounded were carried by helicopter to the hospital twenty-four hours a day. Many recovered at the field hospitals from their injuries and were then sent back to their units. During 1966, the Medical Corps treated over a million South Vietnamese civilians, as well as nearly 6,400 wounded Marines and sailors.

Chaplains were an integral part of the field hospital. The continual flow of wounded meant a constant need for their presence. Many Marines died in the caring arms of a Navy chaplain. Chaplains also made daily visits to the men recuperating in the wards, often helping them write letters home. If at all possible, the chaplain would get word back to the Marine's unit concerning the condition of their wounded comrade.

On December 9, 1966, Father Vincent officially reported for duty at 1st Medical Battalion. While he accepted the assignment, he longed to be with his infantrymen on the front. Chaplain Casazza remembered, "He did not like the Medical Battalion. Naturally, he wanted to be with the men; but they all did, even his commanding officer came to me and tried to persuade me to leave him there."

Father Vincent mentioned the transfer in a letter to his family:

> Not too long ago, I was transferred from 1/7 to our hospital. The work is of a different type but very gratifying. Time passes by just as quickly here as at Battalion and I therefore cannot write as often as I would like.

He was not the only chaplain assigned to the 200-bed hospital; after Christmas, Chaplain Victor Krulak was also stationed with him. Like Father Vincent, Krulak was coming from a combat unit, the 3rd Battalion, 5th Marines. At the hospital, they worked side by side almost twenty-four hours a day. They lived in the same hootch, but rarely got more than four hours sleep a night. Their work alternated between receiving the wounded and visiting patients in the ward. During this draining and hectic schedule, even while eating four times a day, each man lost more than twenty pounds.

Father Vincent already had a lanky build, but now his tanned faced was drawn and his piercing blue eyes were set deep under his brow. He was still quite strong and fit, even though his age became somewhat exaggerated as he approached his 38th birthday and his crewcut hair became more gray. Lieutenant Commander David Taft, Navy doctor and Chief of General Surgery at First Medical, commented that the chaplain reminded him physically of the El Greco painting, "Saint Martin Dividing the Cloak." Both figures were thin, yet strong-willed and determined. Such a characterization would have pleased Father Vincent.

As on the field, Father Vincent's presence at 1st Medical meant more than physical and psychological help. As a Roman Catholic priest, he could also offer the sacraments. For Catholics, the sacraments are not merely beautiful prayers and symbolic gestures. They are effective means of physical and spiritual healing which the priest, by virtue of his ordination, can offer to souls. For a Catholic, the presence of a priest, especially in times of sorrow or difficulty, is a consolation beyond description.

The most common sacraments that Father Vincent and his brother priests offered to the men in Vietnam were Confession, or the Sacrament of Reconciliation, and the Anointing of the Sick, at that time known as Extreme Unction. For young men facing death on a daily basis, Confession was a great consolation. No matter what sins they had committed, they could receive the assurance of God's forgiveness and friendship, allowing them to go into battle with a feeling of readiness and confidence. For those who were seriously wounded or dying, the Anointing of the Sick united them more closely to the suffering and death of the Lord, giving them the moral and psychological strength to accept whatever God had allowed to happen in their lives, building them up in faith and the hope of resurrection.

Lieutenant Jospeh L. LaHood, a Navy doctor, commented on the gentle and effective way Father Vincent carried out his pastoral duties.

> I am a doctor and after a year in Vietnam saw much. But never had I ever seen such dedication and selflessness, not as a sticky 'piety' but as a 'way.' For the hundreds of cigarettes he held for the wounded, many of whom could no longer reach their hands to their lips, and for the hundreds of letters he

wrote and helped to write for his men, the Marines will never forget that he was one of them, this priest of God, is a hero.

There was no question among all of us that God had endowed this man with a unique compassion, insight, and humility. What an example he was to the fighting men he served; how subtly he indicated, without words, that Christ was there! He was a legend.

Krulak recalled Father Vincent's pastoral care of a young corpsman brought to the hospital with severe burns. The corpsman's body was burned to the nerves. His own training told him he was terminal. He asked to see a Catholic priest and go to Confession before his death. Father Vincent heard the young man's confession and asked him if there was anything he wanted. There was: a beer. Capodanno immediately went to the officers' club and got the beer for him, then stayed with him and held him until he died.

Petty Officer George W. Reichert, a Navy Hospital Corpsman at 1st Medical, described the day-to-day action at the hospital and the deeds of the two chaplains:

> I worked in the Admission and Sorting (A&S) section at First Med. Whenever a helicopter came in with casualties both chaplains usually showed up in A&S. Part of our standard procedure was to cut off all the clothing of the injured Marines to allow us to completely examine them. We then covered them with blankets. Father Capodanno always carried a four-inch hunting knife that he used to help cut off the clothing. He would assist us in turning and positioning patients. He and Chaplain Krulak had the ability to quickly reassure and comfort each casualty while allowing us plenty of room to administer to their physical needs. I remember a number of times when a severely injured patient would be surrounded by doctors and corpsmen and I would see Father's hand quickly pass through the mob and anoint the person.

One of the patients who received care at 1st Medical was Sergeant Thomas K. Gill, assigned to D Company, 1st Battalion, 5th Marines. He recalled meeting Father Vincent while he was recovering from his wounds:

I had been wounded, and my first meeting with the good Father was when he came to my cot in the ward and gave me a carton of Salem cigarettes. In fact he gave a carton to every patient in the ward regardless of religion. When he went to a Marine several cots from me, the Marine was in excruciating pain from serious burns over his body, Fr. Capodanno left the ward momentarily and returned with a small bottle of brandy (1 oz.), seeing this I jokingly asked if he had any more. This is when he came to my cot and we had our first conversation.

Several days later, while at the hospital Fr. Capodanno asked me to help say the Gospel (Palm Sunday). This was during March 1967.

Even though Father Vincent was stationed at the field hospital, his bond with the 7th Marines remained unbroken and he took every opportunity to visit them during their operations. From January to May, 3rd Battalion, 7th Marines was assigned to the Duc Pho area about seventy miles south of Chu Lai, for operation "DeSoto." Frequently, Father Vincent arrived by medical-evacuation helicopter, staying a few days at a time, to say Mass and visit the front line troops.

Captain Francis V. White, the Operations Officer for 3/7, remembered that Father Vincent was the only Catholic chaplain who would visit the troops in the isolated and dangerous area of Duc Pho during "DeSoto." Captain White described the combat situation as a "hot area. We had a lot of action all the time. The men needed a chaplain, and he [Father Vincent] was there."

During his many visits to the men at Duc Pho, Father Vincent also met Lieutenant John D. Murray, Executive Officer of M Company, 3rd Battalion, 5th Marines. Murray was a short, stocky, bull-dog type of Marine, a real leader who had seen a lot of action. In a few months, when Father Vincent would be transferred to the 5th Marines, he and Murray would be stationed together.

Whether in the field or at a field hospital, a chaplain is constantly being asked tough questions. "Why did my buddy have to die? Why didn't I die instead of him?" "If God is a good God, how can there be such evil?"

No chaplain can explain away all the miseries of life and war, but his loving presence among his men can be itself an answer. Christ did not simply take away all suffering, but became man, sharing with men everything except sin. As St. Paul writes, "he emptied himself, taking the form of a slave." This mystery of love is the Christian response to suffering and death. Father Vincent gave the witness of Christ's self-emptying every day of his service in Vietnam. In place of bitterness and despair before suffering, he gave his Marines an example of faith and love. He endured the same trials, but always stood ready to offer a compassionate ear, a kind word, a helping hand.

Father Vincent gave many homilies at Mass and spoke at many services on the theme of suffering, and the pain of losing a close friend and fellow Marine. Four of his sermons, offering powerful insights into this man, have survived in various states of completion.

The first sermon was transcribed from a documentary film titled *A Face of War*. The movie was filmed during the summer of 1966 and depicted the thoughts and actions of the Marines of M Company, 3/7. Father Vincent appeared in one scene saying Mass and delivering the following homily:

> Any bit of joy or happiness that we have here is but a taste of the eternal happiness we're going to have in heaven. But in order to achieve that eternal life in heaven, we must go through the process that we have come to call death. God has given us life that we should live it fully, live it completely, live it happily. God chooses the minute called [unclear] death and uses various circumstances to achieve that. O Lord, hear my prayer. Grant us pardon, absolution, and remission of our sins. The Lord be with you and bring you to life everlasting, Amen.

Father Vincent's sermons were usually short due to the lack of time the men had for religious services. Also, it was dangerous to gather a large group in one place for fear of attack. The longest known talk he gave was during his time with the 7th Marines, on the occasion of the dedication of a new command post and the birthday of the battalion.

> Belief in Christ brings with it a deeply rooted sense of the primacy and urgency of now. Not last year or next year, but now.
>
> Each of us has been given talents and ability by Almighty God. We should ask ourselves if we are using these to the best

of our ability. If we don't use them here, chances are we'll not use them elsewhere either. There will always be an excuse.

And it is now that we must consider and appreciate and review our own talents and gifts we have received from the hand of God himself. Properly understood we can be proud of them, but never haughty about them. They are given to us for our own benefit and that of others.

Putting this into the very present tense, we should not look down upon the Vietnamese because they do not have all the gifts and blessings we ourselves have.

What is required of us is the patient *and* intelligent use of our obvious superiority in so many fields. Not as if we ourselves are solely responsible for these gifts but as instruments of God who has given these gifts to us for our own benefit and for the benefit of others as well.

We are not here to engender a feeling of jealousy because of what we have or hatred because we use our gifts perhaps in a very obnoxious way.

We can be compared to adults and the VN to children, but both created by God who is vitally interested in both.

Because of the extremely limited material and spiritual gifts the VN have, we can say they are the least of Christ's brethren. . . .

The Regimental birthday and the dedication of the new CP represent fitting occasion for each of us to do a little analyzing to see if we are using here and now the gifts God has given us in the way he intends for us to use them.

Lord God, Heavenly Father, we ask your blessing on our new CP and the entire BN that we may serve you with faith, our country with loyalty and our BN with courage.

Through your grace and blessing may each of us contribute a spirit of kindness and mature understanding for each other and for the Vietnamese people among whom we are now living.

And Lord God, with pride in the sacrifice and sadness at their absence, we ask your mercy for those of 1/7 who have died. Through your blessing may we be ever inspired by their sacrifice and mindful of the debt we owe them and their families. Keep them in your love and mercy, O Lord, and keep them in our memories that they may be to us a standard for our own efforts.

On this day of dedication, God our Father, we beg your blessing on our new CP and all the members of the BN, both living and dead.

We ask this through Jesus Christ your Son, Our Lord. Amen.

And finally in the words of Paul the Apostle we say: May the grace of Our Lord Jesus Christ, and the love of God, and the fellowship of the Holy Spirit be with us all forever. Amen.

Another homily, written in Father Vincent's hand and difficult to follow because it is incomplete, mentions the complex moral issues of war:

Easily made decisions — only black & white — take on new depth — recognize lrge grey area where we do must of our living — most of our groping. Unfortunately, in grey area where we also experience mst of our religious confusion. . .We received the tiny seed that we mst nourish so it will grow into great tree of Faith. Today's Mass prayer — How do it in a combat zone? Disobedient? Guilty of murder? If only black and white — only confusion. . . . To defend property — life & our way of life. Everyone has these rights. A Democratic way of life based on belief in God has . . . right to defend itself from atheism.

A final homily was scribbled into Father Vincent's pocket calendar book and was written for a memorial service:

At an event such as this . . . our minds groan amid the tragedies & complexities of life looking for an answer. It is with hesitation that we accept the fact: there is no easy answer, there is no glib answer. We are human beings & our views . . . are ltd because of our human limitations. . . . Somehow these events have a meaning, that somehow they work for the good of the persons involved. We cannot fully comprehend how but only that they do.

During his time with 1st Medical, Father Vincent realized the end of his tour of duty was fast approaching — only four months away, in April 1967. While the practice of extending was uncommon, it was possible. The normal rotation was such that chaplains were assigned to a stateside billet after a tour in Vietnam and then, if desired, the chaplain could request another assignment with the Marines in Vietnam. Few chaplains ever applied to extend and even fewer had their request approved. But, Father Vincent knew his call was to serve the Marines in Vietnam; he truly loved his work with the Grunt Marines. He set about seeking an extension of his tour of duty.

Major Ray Savage recalled his reaction to the news of Father Vincent's intention to extend:

> He also mentioned that he had requested an extension of his tour of duty in RVN. Only by knowing him personally could I understand him, or anyone else in their right mind, extending in RVN. Total dedication, a firm faith, and a desire to serve his fellow Marines had to be the explanation.

On January 4, 1967, Father Vincent completed the necessary paperwork to extend his tour by six months. He sent his request to Major General Herman Nickerson, Jr., the Commanding General of the 1st Marine Division, and not through the chaplain chain of command. Chaplain Casazza noted that "He got the extension and, to this day, I do not know how. He did not get the extension through my headquarters." The request was approved on January 9. Ten days later, when he returned from a week's vacation in Hong Kong with Major Fitzgerald, he joyfully received the news that he was going to stay. Father Vincent wrote home the following day to relate the news and also to announce that he would be given a thirty-day leave in April and would come home for part of it. As it turned out, he was not able to go on leave until the first week of May. He wrote to his family at the end of March 1967 to let them know his itinerary.

First on the agenda was a retreat in Manila. A retreat is a short time taken out of one's usual routine to rest and pray. In the Gospel, Christ would from time to time call his apostles away to a quiet place. He also advised all his followers to go into their rooms and pray to their Father who sees in secret. A retreat means taking time to focus on the one thing necessary in life — our communion with God. Anyone can and should make a retreat from time to time, but for priests it is absolutely essential. Their ministry must arise from their intimate friendship with Christ, a friendship cultivated by the time they spend with Him in prayer.

During his short time in Manila, Father Vincent had the opportunity to meet with his old classmate and friend, Father John

Rich. Father Rich recounted that Father Vincent wanted to stay in Vietnam because it "energized him," allowing him to use his talents and abilities to the fullest. In his conversations with Father Rich, Father Vincent spoke also of the questions and concerns he had dealing with the moral issues of the war. Father Vincent showed his awareness of the concrete problems facing the men in his care. He and Father Rich discussed the ways in which a chaplain could provide them with consolation and guidance.

Following his retreat, Father Vincent returned briefly to Chu Lai, then visited old friends in Taiwan and Honolulu. Toward the end of May, he arrived in the United States and stayed with his sister Pauline and her family, making use of the upstairs guestroom with a view overlooking tree-lined Clinton Avenue.

Father Vincent's time at home was not like his many other visits. His sister Pauline recalled it was a somber time. He did not want any parties and he did not go out to visit friends. Pauline noted, "When he came back in June (from Vietnam) he was a changed person; he was not Vin any more." James Capodanno also noticed the difference in his brother:

> It was the first time I saw a change in Vincent. He had changed tremendously. His hair was gray. He would be sitting right across from us, but his mind was in Vietnam. He couldn't wait until he got back to Vietnam.

His sister, Gloria Holman, reflected that "his mind was out there — back with his men. He was very deep in thought and prayer."

The one party which the family had at Pauline's house was not the usual relaxed evening. A few of the priests who came discussed the war and expressed their support of the Vietnam War protests which at that time were picking up momentum. The conversation clearly upset Father Vincent. He took his brother into the kitchen and told him that the priests did not know what was happening in Vietnam.

The anti-war climate he discovered in the United States and the growing lack of support for the brave men he knew in Vietnam brought on a profound melancholy in Father Vincent. His desire to be with his men and care for them increased in direct proportion to what he saw as their rejection by society. While his family could see his suffering, they were not fully able to understand and sympathize. There was no relief for him but to return to his men.

On June 6, 1967, a Western Union telegram arrived modifying Father Vincent's orders and requiring him to depart New Jersey sooner than expected. His time with his family had been brief. In the hasty round of good-byes to be said, there was hardly time to reflect on the possibility that these would be the last moments they had together. Three days later he flew back to Vietnam from Norton Air Force Base in San Bernardino, California. During the layover in Okinawa, Father Vincent was fortunate to meet Major Fitzgerald, who was on his way back to the States. The two friends had only a half-hour to visit. They would not see each other again.

The Vietnam War, like all wars, was fought to conquer and destroy the enemy in order to achieve a military goal; but military goals are not ends in themselves. They are set in light of some higher goal — in this case, the defense of freedom. For Father Vincent, the United States' involvement in Vietnam was a justified and ethical undertaking. He firmly believed that the war was fought in order to free the Vietnamese from Communist oppression. He had understood the tragedy of Communist rule in China and believed the freedom for which the Vietnamese people longed could be won by working with them.

In two letters, Father Vincent briefly described his support for the troops and the war effort. He wrote to the Military Ordinariate that, "Militarily, things are going along much as you read about them in the papers. The morale is good and the morals in many, many instances are nothing short of exemplary and inspiring. Really." In another letter he wrote: "The war here is going along as you read about it in the papers. Eventually and ultimately, the Viet Cong will be forced back and peace and prosperity will come to this section, this very beautiful section, of the world."

Captain Thomas E. Byrne, Supply Officer at the 1st Engineer Battalion, also recalled the support Father Vincent gave to the troops and the war effort. Captain Byrne stated:

Since killing people in war is a deadly serious business, the hint of possible immorality in this regard would be most unsettling to men who value their souls and God's approval and blessings on their duty.

Two Marines asked Father what was going on in the USA. Father Vince explained that he had recently returned from a Stateside leave and that there was opposition to the war in the United States, even among priests and religious in the Church. They (at home) asked him how he could support the war.

He told them, and he told us, that the opponents simply didn't understand what was going on in Viet Nam; that they (the opponents) were being misled. Father assured the Marines that what they were doing was right and justified and that they could be proud of their service.

I still take comfort in Father's defense of our efforts in Viet Nam. The Church became more or less a "hostile environment" for the veterans of that war and, although I knew we were right, that Navy chaplain put a confirming stamp of approval on our war effort that affects me in a positive way to this very day.

As soon as he arrived in Vietnam, Father Vincent sent a letter home detailing his duties for the next several weeks:

I am going, eventually, to the 1st Battalion, 5th Marines. For the next three weeks or so, I am going to be filling in for two priests who are going on retreat. I'll be here for ten days (at the hospital where I was before returning to the States) and then go, also for ten days, to my old unit, 1st BN-7th MAR. Sometime around 1 July I will go to 1st BN-5th MAR.

His new assignment was in one of the fiercest combat zones in Vietnam during that summer: the Que Son Valley, about twenty-five kilometers northwest of the Tam Ky area. In the hills of Nui Loc Son, the Marines battled the entrenched North Vietnamese Army (NVA). There were two types of forces in the North Vietnamese military. The NVA was a well trained and heavily armed force responsible for the major battles fought against American troops. The other force was known as the Viet Cong (VC), consisting of recruited farmers and laborers from the north who possessed no professional training as soldiers. While the NVA was a force to contend with, the VC did little serious damage to the American forces.

During the summer of 1967, the Marines engaged in operations "Union" and "Union II." The build up for "Union" had started early in January: American forces came from the Da Nang and Chu Lai areas, with the Fifth Marines making up part of the combined force. Operation "Union" lasted through April and May 1967, and resulted in 583 Marine casualties — 110 killed, 473 wounded. The death toll for the enemy was 810.

The bloodshed continued with "Union II" in late May and early June, the battle with the NVA having moved closer to the Tam Ky area. Again, the enemy casualties were high: 701 killed. The Marines lost 110 men with 241 wounded. Even with such heavy losses, the enemy was determined to build up replacement forces in the Que Son Valley in order to regain military control and Communist domination of the area. Throughout the summer, the Que Son Valley was a scene of violent fighting. This was the situation that Chaplain Capodanno found when he reported to 1st Battalion, 5th Marines on July 3, 1967.

The 1st Battalion command post was located on the top of Hill 51 on the eastern bank of the Ly Ly River near the village of Que Son. The battalion commander was Colonel Peter Hilgartner, a tall, lean, disciplined Marine who commanded his front-line men with stern authority, keeping them battle-ready for a meeting with the NVA.

While Father Vincent was specifically assigned as the chaplain for 1/5, as a Catholic priest he served all the Catholic Marines of the 5th Regiment. He also voluntarily joined Colonel Hilgartner and the other officers in the nightly task of "walking the lines." Being in a tense and potentially volatile combat zone, the posts which surrounded and protected the battalion were critical to defense. "Walking the lines" meant visiting the Marines in these outlying areas to ensure that the defenses were ready at all times throughout the night.

Corporal Tim J. Hanley, I Company 3/5, described how surprised he and his fellow Marines were when Father Vincent first visited them on the line. No chaplain had ever come to visit them in the outposts. Because Father Vincent was out in the field, he was there to help Corporal Hanley deal with the news of the death of his niece. Said Hanley: "He got down in the mud; he wanted to share your experiences and problems. He was an easy guy to open up to."

Father Vincent was now as busy at night as he was during the day, leaving him little time for sleep; but wherever his Marines were, that was where he wanted to be. Corporal Bob Gerton, A Company 1/5, one of the Marines the priest visited at the front, recalled, "No matter what was going on he would be there and that's what was important in Vietnam." Once again, Father Vincent was following Bishop Ford's dictum, "to suffer with." His line ministry contributed to his already great popularity and effectiveness among the Marines and earned the respect and admiration of Colonel Hilgartner.

Lieutenant Frederick Smith, Platoon Leader of I Company 3/5, met Father Vincent for the first time at a late-night poker game. Smith noted that Father Vincent was not only an accomplished card player, but also:

> "[He was a] unique man . . . he just had a personality and a demeanor which enlisted a great deal of affection and respect and almost instantaneously. I never knew anybody who had anything but the highest regard for Father Capodanno. He was a man who had the courage of a lion and the faith of a martyr."

Like their buddies in the 7th, the Marines of the 5th commented that Father Vincent was "one of us, he was a Marine." Corporal Hanley stated, "He was not just an attachment. You felt sometimes that some chaplains and corpsman do not want to be there and would rather be on a clean Navy ship or visiting a hospital." Father Vincent, however, lived and worked right alongside the men. Corporal John Scafidi, K Company 3/5, remembered that the chaplain willingly shared the same hardships as any grunt. He could have stayed in the rear, but he carried a forty-pound pack, marched in the wet, cold and hot, and stayed right alongside of them. Scafidi further commented: "The task he performed when in the field in a combat situation was to assist the wounded but more important he would assist the dying. Our chaplain was with the grunts, closest to the fighting. Closest to where he would be needed the most."

Corporal Gerlad J. Zimmerman, K Company, 3/5, remembered Father Vincent for his untiring dedication and commented on his effectiveness in the field with "his grunts":

> Father Vin was truly the enlisted men's priest. I remember when I first met Father, it was during mid-August on an Operation in Que Son Valley by the name of Cochise. At the time, I was a radioman for our Company Commander. Father Capodanno was traveling with the Headquarters of our Company — 'Kilo' Company that is. Father enjoyed going to the field to take care of us — his Marines. To continue, Father Vin approached me as we stopped for a short break. As usual, all the 'jarheads' in the area were complaining of sore feet, poor chow (really just the C rations they didn't care for) and I was no exception. One Marine would call to me and say 'Hey, Zimm, would you have any lousy fruit you would want to trade for date pudding?' Of course my answer was, 'I wish I had.' The Chaplain, who I was talking with at the time, reached in his pack (which was as big and heavy as any 'grunt' infantryman would carry) and offered me some peaches. Upon my refusal he took a can opener, opened the peaches, ate a few and again offered them to me. Again, I refused and he said 'Well, I'll just set them here. If you won't enjoy them maybe the flies will.' Of course, after staring at the flies, I thought I had better eat them. That was the kind of person Father Vin was.

Father Vincent, always thinking of the welfare of his grunts, continued writing letters asking his family and friends for needed supplies which would make life easier for his Marines. The following request was written during the summer of 1967:

> Many have asked if there is anything the men can use. Any goodies you can think of will be greatly appreciated. Also this: there is a new product called a SPACE BLANKET made of the same material as space suits. It is blanket shaped, waterproof, heat-proof, cold-proof, light-weight, costs about 8 or 9 dollars and is probably sold in some camping or sports goods stores. If you ever want to send anything at all to the men here, address it FOR THE MARINES followed by the name and address. I will get your package to the men and we will both

write and let you know it has arrived.

Lieutenant Commander Eli Takesian, Presbyterian minister and the 5th Marine Chaplain, was Father Vincent's immediate superior. Chaplain Takesian first heard about the undying dedication of the chaplain from New York City while Father Vincent was on his thirty-day leave in the States. Takesian recalled forming a mental picture of Father Vincent, with whom he would soon serve in the Fifth Marines, picturing him as "a burly Italian, loud, gregarious, back slapper, an extrovert of extroverts."

But Takesian's mental picture of Father Vincent was quite different from the flesh-and-blood reality. His first view was through the raised flaps of a tent as the priest was saying Mass. Takesian noted his serenity and deliberate movements during the Mass. "It [the Mass] was almost like seeing a ballet — the utter grace, sureness. It was mesmerizing." When Takesian met Father Vincent afterwards, he was immediately impressed by the priest's eyes: "His eyes told me everything about him. They were tender eyes, they were sad eyes, friendly eyes, and in their own way they were eyes that were fired by the spirit of God."

Father Vincent was not the burly Italian Takesian expected. Instead, he was soft-spoken, thin, and wiry. He looked more the part of a compassionate priest, which he was, than the zealous Marine officer which Takesian had imagined. The fastidious dresser who never had filled the rough-and-ready image of a missionary had evidently softened with suffering. Father Vincent wore his faded, drab olive Marine utilities like a grunt and not like a spit-and-polish military commander.

Father Vincent wanted to continue to serve the Marines he had grown to love and admire, but he knew that unless he extended again he would be moved in November to a stateside duty station. On July 10, 1967, he sent his extension request for another six months to the Commanding General of the First Marine Division. "I do not desire to leave" was his sole reason for the extension. In early August, Father Vincent received word that his request for a six-month extension was not granted by the Chief of Chaplains, Rear Admiral James W. Kelly.

However, persistent as ever, this denial did not stop him from submitting another request. He wrote to his brother James that his "application for a second six-month extension has been refused. I am now waiting on word in answer to my application for a two-month extension." In a letter written to Colonel Stanley Davis, the 5th Regimental Commander, Father Vincent stated: "I am due to go home in late November or early December. I humbly request that I stay over Christmas and New Year's with my men. I am willing to relinquish my 30 days leave." In his last letter to his family he mentioned to his brother Albert about being turned down again:

> I am fine . . . in good health and spirits. My request to headquarters for another two-month extension of duty here was turned down. . . . I will keep trying. I even offered to forfeit my 30-day rest-and-recreation leave in order to be with the boys at Christmas . . . but my request was not granted. So, it looks like one way or another, I'll be out of the Orient by December. . . .

Father Vincent simply and clearly loved his Marines and wanted to stay with them, especially over the holiday season — always a difficult time for young men to be away from their families.

During the middle of August 1967, Father Vincent was transferred from the 1st Battalion to the 3rd Battalion, 5th Marines. Chaplain Takesian noted that this transfer was made for logistical reasons. He could better serve all three battalions of the regiment if he were more centrally located. The 3rd Battalion was positioned between the 1st and 2nd, and was also only a few hundred yards from regimental headquarters where helicopters were readily available. Chaplain Charles R. Parker, a lieutenant and a Southern Baptist, replaced Father Vincent at 1/5.

Lieutenant Edward B. Burrow, platoon commander in B Company 1/5, remembered the effect Father Vincent's transfer had on him and his men:

> The Marines of the BN [battalion] truly loved him because of the way he was and the confidence which he helped build in each one of us. When I found out that he was going to another BN, I was very sad because the BN didn't want to lose him.

He was such a contributing factor to the morale of the BN that we didn't want to lose him.

During Father Vincent's transfer to the 3rd Battalion, operation "Cochise" was being carried out by both the 1st and 3rd Battalions of the 5th Marines. The operation required the two battalions to be heli-lifted south to the Nui Loc Son area. The mission involved search and destroy sweeps of the area in order to engage the 2nd Division of the NVA, which was gaining in size and strength. While the operation forced a withdrawal of the 2nd Division, there was little actual combat and no tangible defeat of the enemy. The operation officially ended on August 28, 1967. However, the enemy's presence was still a threat to the Que Son Valley, and the growing strength of the NVA caused the 5th Marines to be on constant alert.

Throughout the summer of 1967, and after his transfer to 3/5, Father Vincent continued to meet the demanding schedule he had set for himself. The Masses he offered, the memorial services he led, the innumerable confessions he heard, the around-the-clock counseling, and his constant desire to be with his Grunts, filled his days and left little time for sleeping.

Yet, for all his dedication, Father Vincent was a man of peace and not war. He went in to the field with the Marines not to fight, but to empathize with them and be there for them in their day-to-day problems. Captain Tony Grimm, Staff Officer in 1/5, and Corporal John Scafidi remembered Father Vincent as a dedicated chaplain, who would do anything to be with his grunts in the field. They also recalled that while Father Vincent served with the 5th Marines, he was required to wear a pistol for his protection. In reality, he wore the pistol out of obedience, and for no other reason. Scafidi said:

> Because he went into the field with the grunts, the Battalion commander [Lieutenant Colonel Charles Webster] told him that he had to wear a weapon. He was fearful for his life. You must remember he wasn't trained and he was truly non-combatant. . . . So Chaplain Capodanno [sic] wore a sidearm, a Colt 45 pistol. We all admired our chaplain. Day after day the pistol grew bright orange with neglect for we knew the chaplain would [sic] never use it. Our chaplain was just like the rest

of us — the best of the best. The story goes on; a grunt noticed the 'orange' pistol and told the chaplain, 'You know, Father, it's a shame to let that pistol rust like that.' The chaplain knew that when he finished with it, the pistol would [sic] be recycled to a Marine who would need it in a combat situation. He took the pistol and sat down and cleaned it back to blue and functioning again. Our chaplain wore the cleanest, shiniest pistol and kept it that way knowing he would never use it for anything more than a paperweight.

Though Father Vincent would never pick up a gun or in any way commit an act of aggression, he was nonetheless engaged in warfare. His was a spiritual battle: to stand up and witness to the Gospel even where evil and despair seemed to have the upper hand. His presence on the field, in the front lines, where he was needed most, gave the stamp of authenticity to what he believed and lived. This example was not lost or wasted on the Marines with whom he served. In the final analysis, the weapons Father Vincent carried into battle were those encouraged by St. Paul when he wrote:

> Therefore take the whole armour of God, that you may be able to withstand in the evil day. . . . Stand therefore, having girded your loins with truth, and having put on the breastplate of righteousness, and having shod your feet with the equipment of the Gospel of peace; above all taking the shield of faith, with which you can quench all the flaming darts of the evil one. And take the helmet of salvation, and the word of the Spirit, which is the Word of God.

(Ephesians 6:13–17)

SEMPER FIDELIS

*He who would exercise his power of redeeming to
the utmost limit, as Christ did, must not shrink from
that which awaits all saviours: the cross — passus,
crucifixus est. Souls are won by words, they are won
by example; but above all they are won by sacrifice. In
this conflict it is those that fall who are victorious; the
salvation of the world belongs to the crucified.*

Raoul Plus, S.J.,
Radiating Christ: An Appeal to Militant Catholics

September 4, 1967, was a very hot Labor Day in the United
States. In New York City, temperatures reached a high of 87 de-
grees. It was the kind of day on which a young Vincent
Capodanno would have headed for the local swimming hole.
Throughout the nation, while union leaders rallied locals in support of labor issues, families enjoyed picnics and backyard barbecues on the last official day of summer vacation.

But the lazy holiday feeling of that Labor Day weekend was
misleading. While families and friends enjoyed cool drinks and
laughter in their backyards, on the other side of the globe
450,000 American servicemen continued to face a numbing
sameness in the cities and rice fields of Vietnam. The escalation
in American forces that had peaked in 1965 did not result in a
quick and easy victory. By the fall of 1967, American forces
were suffering more than 100 casualties a day from those killed
or wounded in action. The war dragged on, with casualties
mounting, while television journalism brought the horrors of the
war into the home.

The biggest news out of Vietnam that weekend was the election of General Nguyen Van Thieu as president of South Vietnam, and General Nguyen Cao Ky as vice-president. The Thieu-Ky ticket received 35 percent of the vote, outdistancing ten other slates. The government of the United States had sent twenty-two prominent Americans to observe the election and determine whether the balloting was conducted fairly. In their opinion, it was. If this event was meant to assure the American public that things were moving forward in Vietnam, the reality was quite different, and most Americans were beginning to sense what was called a "credibility gap" between the Johnson administration and the nation.

A grass roots peace movement that had started on college campuses finally caught the attention of important public figures. Dr. Martin Luther King, Jr., who had stayed somewhat in the background on the issue of Vietnam during the civil rights crusade, again criticized the war in a speech at Fire Island, New York. On September 4, George Romney, the moderate Republican governor from Michigan, gave a television interview on the subject of Vietnam. Speaking of a 1965 trip there, he said, "I just had the greatest brainwashing that anyone can get when you go over to Vietnam, not only by the generals, but also by the diplomatic corps over there, and they do a thorough job."

Times had changed since the highly patriotic years following World War II. As the sixties wore on, the fear of Communism and the pressures of the Cold War, which had fueled the conviction to defend democratic governments, began to diminish. On that very Labor Day of 1967, *Time* magazine released its September 8 issue, which stated that in just one summer a dramatic change had occurred in public opinion in regards to Vietnam: "Between Independence Day and Labor Day a profound malaise has gripped the American people."

For families such as the Capodannos, however, the festivities of the weekend and the voices of debate could not diminish the daily awareness that at any moment one of their own might join the growing list of casualties. As they enjoyed the traditional picnics and barbecues of that Labor Day, a subtle uneasiness lay underneath their smiles and conversations, and in the quiet of their hearts they waited and prayed.

The previous weekend had started like any other in Vietnam. From the battalion command post, small platoon-size patrols went into the field on search-and-destroy missions. Guards kept vigil throughout the camp to ensure that gates and outposts were secure. Exhausted Marines tried to sleep through the heat of the day, knowing that the night meant another sleepless duty at a distant listening post close to enemy lines. Helicopters landed, refueled, and took off again; a constant hum from their motors and blades reverberated throughout the camp.

In the midst of this life, so far removed from the comforts of hearth and home, Father Vincent offered oasis to those who were hurting. In quiet places, a step removed from the action, he would stand with head bowed, listening to the confession of a young Marine, receiving into his own heart all the sorrow and fear of the other. The words of absolution, marked by the sign of the cross, were followed by comfort and reassurance that together they would see each other through this time of trial.

Father Vincent would then reach into the big pouch-like pockets of his utilities and present the young man with one of the hundreds of Saint Christopher medals he had ordered for distribution. On the front of the small nickel-sized medal was the image of Saint Christopher carrying the Christ Child across a river, and stamped on the back were the words "Vietnam-1967."

Christopher means "Christ bearer." Such a medal was an appropriate gift from one who bore the suffering of the men he loved so much. Saint Christopher, a saint and martyr of the third century, was a giant of a man who made his living carrying people across a river. One day, a small child asked him for a lift, but as they went forward, the weight of the child grew and grew until Christopher staggered under the burden. Finally reaching the other side, Christopher was astounded to discover that it was Christ he had carried. For Christians, the story of Saint Christopher taught a double lesson of compassion for those who suffer and the reality of Christ's presence in the soul.

Father Vincent's gesture surely conveyed his concern and support for the men under his spiritual guidance, and at the same time it reminded them of their dignity and worth as sons of their

Heavenly Father. To this day, many Marines cherish the Christopher medal given to them by Father Vincent.

Lieutenant Joseph E. Pilon, a Navy doctor, aptly described Father Vincent's way of ministering to the Marines in his care. After the chaplain's death, he wrote to Sister George Marie, S.S.N.D.:

> His audience was always a small group of 20 to 40 Marines gathered together on a hillside, or behind some rocks, hearing confessions — saying Mass. It was almost as though he had decided to leave the 'other 99' in a safe area and go after the one who had gotten in trouble.

In sacraments and signs and simple acts, Father Vincent moved about the Marines bearing Christ's love to them. When day gave way to night, his work was just beginning. His usual routine was to visit the outlying bunkers where squads of four men in each bunker ensured perimeter protection for the command post of the 3rd Battalion, 5th Marines. Bunker duty, so vital to the security of the unit, required constant vigilance. One of the four Marines had to keep watch at all times throughout the night.

Sounds in the jungle are magnified and seem ominously close when a Marine is restless and frightened. In the thick vegetation, the distinction between a human and an animal's noise is difficult. Not surprisingly, Father Vincent's nightly visits to these islands of protection were always welcomed.

In quiet whispers, the men told the chaplain their needs and desires, and shared the news of home-front joys and sorrows. Father Vincent's mere presence was the most comforting factor of all. His division chaplain, David Casazza, once inquired what he did while he was out with the troops. The chaplain replied:

> I am just there with them — I walk with them and sit with them; I eat with them and sleep in the holes with them — and I talk with them — but only when *they* are ready to talk. It takes time, but I never rush them.

Until early each Sunday morning, Father Vincent visited bunker after bunker. Finally, exhausted, he made his way to his tent and found a few hours of sleep before the heat of the day began again.

On Sunday, September 3, Father Vincent celebrated Mass in the three battalions of the 5th Regiment. After several months of serving with the 5th Marines he had his routine down. Early Sunday morning he boarded a helicopter to begin his "circuit-riding" ministry. First he celebrated Mass for the 3rd Battalion, then flew to his old unit at Hill 51, the 1st Battalion. After each Mass, endless lines formed in order to visit with Father Vincent, and he patiently made time for each Marine. After a long helicopter flight to the 2nd Battalion far south of Da Nang in the village of An Hoa of the Tam Ky area, he again celebrated Mass, heard confessions and offered counsel to many.

According to Chaplain Takesian, regimental chaplain for the 5th Marines, after Father Vincent completed his service schedule at the 2nd Battalion, he usually took a helicopter to Da Nang and stayed there both Sunday and Monday nights, returning to his home unit, the 3rd Battalion, on Tuesday morning with a supply helicopter from Da Nang. Chaplain Takesian assumed, therefore, that on the night of September 3 his colleague was in Da Nang. But instead of taking a helicopter to Da Nang, Father Vincent had stayed in the Tam Ky area and celebrated another Mass. The 2nd Battalion, 11th Marines, a 105mm Howitzer Battalion, was supporting the 5th Marines from positions located near the 2nd Battalion, 5th Marines. Father Vincent visited with this battalion and offered Mass at the battalion command post.

Corporal Joe Trischetti was one of the Marines of 2/11 and an altar server at this final Mass. He recalled the location of the Mass and the main points of Father Vincent's final homily:

> The sermon was contemporary for people in our position. He spoke of trying to grasp some pleasure in life. Since what most of our young eyes were seeing at that time was just the misery of life. He urged the men to take their R&Rs when they were eligible. . . . This last Mass that he offered was at the bottom of Hill 327. . . . I was an altar boy and for seats we utilized empty wooden ammunition boxes for 105mm-howitzers and 4.2" mortar shells. The sky was a beautiful blue that day, and the sun was bright. I guess there was [sic] about fifteen of us young kids there that day for the service.

After Mass, Father Vincent was taken by helicopter back to his home unit, 3/5. His full day was finished.

This Sunday was the eve of elections in South Vietnam. The North Vietnamese Army (NVA) would most likely try to disrupt the election process. Father Vincent thought back to the previous September when he sat on a hillside near Chu Lai with Major Dick Alger, Intelligence Officer for the 7th Marine Regiment, observing the shelling of the South Vietnamese citizens as they tried to vote. He knew that the North Vietnamese Army was amassing strength since their defeat in the Que Son Valley during operation "Cochise" the previous month. Perhaps his intuition of an impending battle explains his unscheduled trip back to 3/5. He had access to official military intelligence that advised of a possible enemy attack. The notification stated:

> The Marines anticipated that the Communists would try to increase their strength in this area during this period, since it corresponded with the time of the South Vietnamese national elections, as well as preparations for the fall rice harvest. At the beginning of September, intelligence sources reported that elements of all three regiments of the NVA division (2nd North Vietnamese Army Division) had moved into the area. There were increasing indications that these enemy units planned offensive actions to disrupt the elections in Que Son District.

Father Vincent stayed with his unit that night. He prayed into the early hours of the morning, finally catching a few hours of sleep. The heat and the insects didn't disturb him — six years in Taiwan and sixteen months in the jungles of Vietnam had hardened him to tropical climates. That night he was kept from a deep and restful sleep by the premonition of what the morning would bring. He prayed for the souls of the men who would lose their lives if there were a battle. He had seen a lot of action during his time in Vietnam, but he hadn't yet got used to seeing his brother Marines killed and wounded. If the enemy did attack the next day he wanted to be there where they needed him most.

Operation "Swift" began on Monday, September 4, as just a routine maneuver. Eight miles southwest of the city of Thang Binh, Captain Robert F. Morgan's D Company, 1/5 was conducting screening sweeps around the small village of Dong Son. A sweep was a standard "search-and-destroy" mission which attempted to flush out and destroy the enemy, thus ensuring the village would be protected from enemy interference during the national election and rice harvesting. The sweeps were uneventful until 4:30 a.m., when unexpectedly the skies lit up with enemy mortars and bullet tracers. The North Vietnamese Army (NVA) had found the Marines, and what started out as commonplace military activity in Thang Binh District soon became a test of force and faith.

The NVA had a distinct advantage over the surprised and temporarily disorganized Company D. Calling for air strikes from an armed UH-1E helicopter (HUIE), the company used a strobe light to mark its position, but the light attracted more accurate fire from the enemy. The confident NVA began to infiltrate the western segments of the company perimeter. Some time after 6:30 a.m., Captain Morgan was mowed down by the NVA's automatic weapons. The company was in need of reinforcements and the wounded Marines needed immediate transport to a battalion aid station.

Lieutenant Colonel Peter L. Hilgartner, Commander of 1st Battalion, 5th Marines, responded at 6:55 a.m., by committing Company B to the battle. By 9:14 a.m, twenty-six Marines were confirmed killed in action. Operation "Swift" was rapidly becoming more than a typical search-and-destroy sweep.

In the early hours of the battle, few details were known at 3/5's command post. No one could have predicted the size and seriousness of the situation. Father Vincent got word on the action and, according to Captain Ed B. Burrow, a staff officer in 1/5, he joined the 5th Marine leadership for the early morning briefing on the battle at 1st Battalion's Combat Operation Center. Burrow noted:

> During my brief he [Capodanno] sat there very cool and calm and didn't say a word. But he did take a few notes on what I had said. When he left the briefing which was at 'O dark thirty,' he looked at me and said, 'It's not going to be easy out there.'

Father Vincent returned to 3/5 by helicopter and waited with his unit in case the companies of the 3rd Battalion were called into action.

The fighting at Dong Son continued through the early morning. At 8:20 a.m., Company B arrived in support of the severely crippled Company D. In order to break the enemy's entrenched defensive line, HUIE's delivered 400 pounds of CS gas on enemy positions. With this action, the NVA began a retreat north across the Ly Ly River. But when helicopters arrived a short time later to transport the wounded of Company D, the attack resumed with intensity, grounding the helicopters.

At 9:25 a.m., Lieutenant Colonel Hilgartner requested the assistance of two companies from the 3rd Battalion. Lieutenant Colonel Charles B. Webster, Commanding Officer of the 3rd Battalion, responded to the request by assigning both Companies M and K to be heli-lifted to the combat medical aid station, which also served as the combat landing zone.

Knowing that there were wounded at the aid station and in the field, Father Vincent wanted to go with the two companies. He had spent all of the previous week with Company M, so he knew the Marines and the company commander, Lieutenant John D. Murray. Richard L. Kline, 1st Sergeant of Company M, recalled Father Vincent's request to accompany Company M:

> Chaplain Capodanno had initially approached me about the possibility of going out on a Company Search and Destroy mission with Mike [M] Company. [I] told him, this was unheard of for a chaplain to go out with a Line Company, where he would be exposed to enemy small arms fire. I personally denied his request, to the extent that I did not even inform the Company Commander of the Chaplain's request. However, Chaplain Capodanno informed me that he would see the Battalion Commander for his approval. Evidently, this was approved somewhere along the line, because he did end up in Mike Company operation in September, 1967.

Father Vincent sought the permission of Lieutenant Colonel Webster, who reluctantly gave his consent for the chaplain's transport with Company M to the aid station. Marine UH-34D helicopters began immediately transporting the two companies to the landing zone and the medical aid station. Chaplain Eli Takesian also wanted to go into the field to assist the wounded and dying. He requested permission from Colonel Stanley Davis,

Regimental Commander of the 5th Marines, to join his former unit, 3/5, as they began their movement into the field. While Takesian knew that 3/5 was Father Vincent's responsibility, he assumed that the priest was in Da Nang as was his usual routine on a Monday morning. When he asked permission from Lieutenant Colonel Webster, Takesian learned that Father Vincent had already left at 10 a.m. with elements of Company M. Takesian recalled his reaction to the news:

> I questioned whether he should go out with a company; but felt relieved when told that it was now a multi-company operation (larger than a battalion) and his mission was to reach the hastily-set-up medical aid unit, to minister to the dying and wounded. The rest of 3/5 was scheduled to chopper out at 1600 [4:00 PM], and I went with them.

According to an official report, the helicopters carrying the Marines of Companies K and M, including Father Vincent, were to land just east of Hill 63 and the Dong Son village, where Companies B and D were fighting. But, according to Chaplain Takesian, the ground fire was so intense that the helicopters were forced to land some distance from the landing zone and the aid station. Official records noted that the helicopters "landed four kilometers east-northeast of Dong Son." The landing location was near route 543 and the village of Dinh An.

Shortly after noon, Companies K and M began to hike to Dong Son. The two companies advanced in column through slightly hilly terrain covered with low vegetation and surrounded by rice paddies. It was a typical hot, humid day with the temperature in the 90s. As on so many days, courage and apprehension ran high.

Father Vincent was with the command post of Company M, between the 1st and the 2nd Platoons. Just before the march, he gave General Absolution and distributed Communion to all who sought the sacraments. Wartime knows no hard-and-fast rules on Christian reconciliation, and Father Vincent provided a spiritual embrace to whoever requested it. Corporal John Scafidi, Company K, recalled the event:

> The reason for our calm, cool, total business attitude was we were given General Absolution along with Communion by

Chaplain Capodanno just as we first started to walk that morning. I remember seeing him giving Communion before to those who wanted it, but not the entire formation.

Lieutenant Colonel Hilgartner received intelligence reports from both scouts in the field and Major Alger at the Combat Operations Center that a large NVA force was directly in front of Companies K and M. Hilgartner changed the tactical formation from an advancing column to an attack formation. As a protective flanking measure, Company M moved to the right of Company K's "V" formation. Hilgartner then ordered "fixed bayonets." The NVA were in an "L"-shaped entrenched position near the village of Chau Lam.

At 2:45 p.m., as the 1st Platoon of Company M descended the crest of a hill, the enemy attacked with sudden and lethal force. Within moments a heavy volume of automatic small arms and mortar fire engulfed the defenseless and exposed platoon. The 2nd Platoon of Company M maneuvered along the base of the hill to support the 1st Platoon. The command post of Company M, where Father Vincent was stationed, took position in a crater slightly behind the crest of the hill. The devastating attack continued just over the crest of the hill as the leadership of the command post tried to determine where the enemy was and how best to repel them. The hill acted as a natural defense and offered relative safety for Father Vincent and those in the command post. During the ambush, Corporal Thomas Forgas was also at the command post with Father Vincent. Forgas, a terrified twenty year old, remembered the chaplain's calming words and presence.

While Father Vincent was physically safe, he still heard the cries and anguish of his wounded men just a few hundred yards away over the top of the hill. The sounds of explosions, gunfire, and human agony rifled through his very heart and soul. Despite his deep faith and his training, nothing could ease the anguish he felt for his men.

The vicious, close-combat battle continued without any relief for the outnumbered Marines. The 1st Platoon tried to regroup at the top of the hill in order to form a secure perimeter. Meanwhile, the 2nd Platoon, under Lieutenant Edward L. Blecksmith, was pinned down at the base of the hill; the Marines were clinging to the dirt in the fear of being detected and shot if they moved or tried to fire back. PFC Stephen A. Lovejoy, the radio operator, made a desperate attempt to contact the command post with the announcement, "We can't hold out here. We are being wiped out! There are wounded and dying all around."

At the command post, Father Vincent heard the message. He leaped from the crater behind the hill and ran towards the 2nd Platoon. Lovejoy was trying to get to the top of the hill with his bulky radio but was pinned down by heavy automatic fire and mortar explosions. The AN/PRC-25, the standard radio used in Vietnam by the Marines, was a heavy but essential piece of equipment. Somehow he had to get the radio and himself up to the perimeter. At that moment, Lovejoy looked up and saw Father Vincent running toward him through a hail of bullets. Father Vincent grabbed one of the straps of the radio and together they crawled to the top of the hill with the radio. They had to stop for cover twice before they reached the relative safety of the defensive line. Lovejoy remembered the event with emotion: "I would never have made it up the hill alive without the Chaplain's aid." No sooner had he deposited Lovejoy on top of the hill than Father Vincent immediately went back down to continue helping. On his first trip, he went to the side of Corporal Stephen Connell, who was near death, and gave him the Last Rites.

The NVA continued their aggressive attack on the 2nd Platoon, at one point totally encircling their position. To repel the enemy, the command post ordered CS (tear) gas dropped directly on the 2nd Platoon. The Marines were issued masks for protection against such defensive tactics. Father Vincent put his mask on and continued comforting the wounded until he noticed that one Marine had left his gas mask at the bottom of the hill. Spontaneously, he gave his mask to the choking Marine and refused those offered by other Marines. He even resisted sharing their masks with them. He simply said, "You need it for fighting, I'm all right."

Both PFC Julio Rodríguez and Corporal Keith J. Rounseville commented on Father Vincent's heroic and constant maneuvering to help the wounded. Rodríguez remembered the scene vividly:

This is when I first spotted Father Capodanno. He was carrying a wounded Marine. After he brought him into the relative safety of our perimeter, he continued to go back and forth giving Last Rites to dying men and bringing in wounded Marines. He made many trips, telling us to 'stay cool; don't panic.'

Rounseville concurred with Rodríguez. He recalled:

I did not see Chaplain Capodanno during the first moments of intense fighting. When I did see him, he was jumping over my hole, all the while exposing himself to enemy machine gun fire to try and give aid to a wounded Marine. Chaplain Capodanno looked and acted cool and calm, as if there wasn't an enemy in sight. As he reached the wounded Marine, Chaplain Capodanno lay down beside him and gave him aid and verbal encouragement and telling [sic] him medical help was on the way.

Father Vincent's valiant actions inspired others in the nearly hand-to-hand combat conditions. Corporal David Brooks, 2nd Platoon, stated, "The chaplain's example of action gave courage to everyone who observed him and sparked others to action. Quite a few more people would have died if not for him."

Sergeant Lawrence D. Peters, Squad Leader of the 2nd Platoon, also gave heroic service that day. Even after being wounded twice, Peters exposed himself to devastating enemy fire in order to point out where the NVA were infiltrating the lines of defense. Mortally wounded in the chest, Peters lay dying on the battlefield. Corporal Brooks saw Father Vincent move to the exposed area where Peters was lying. As he ran toward Peters, Father Vincent was hit by the shrapnel of a mortar that exploded about twenty meters away. Spots of blood were seen on his right shoulder as he held his right arm stiffly to his side. Finally, the priest made his way to Peters' side. He prayed the Our Father with Peters, who was Russian Orthodox, and stayed at his side for about five minutes until he died.

Disregarding his injury, Father Vincent continued to seek out the wounded. After he left Sergeant Peters, he worked his way over to five other Marines, bandaging their wounds and giving them comfort. Corporal Brooks noted that Father Vincent told those Marines, "Jesus said, 'Have Faith.'" Lieutenant Blecksmith also heard Father Vincent consoling the wounded with the expression, "Jesus is the truth and the life."

Corporal George Phillips, Squad Leader of 1st Platoon, noted the care and respect Father Vincent had for all those to whom he ministered in the field:

> He was determined to do what he was there to do, he was not going to let those people [the enemy] interfere with his business. He would not get down because he wanted to look at them [the wounded] straight in the eyes. People were yelling at him 'Father get down.' Guys were getting machine-gunned lying on the ground. But, Father Capodanno wanted to calm the wounded by looking them in the eyes.

Sergeant Howard Manfra, 2nd Platoon, was wounded five times and lay dazed and in severe pain on an exposed slope between the crossfire of two NVA automatic weapons. Other Marines, who were in a slight depression just off the knoll, tried to recover Manfra and bring him to safety, but the danger was too great. Heedless of his own safety, Father Vincent managed to reach the sergeant, calm him and drag him into the depression. Corporal Rounseville then called out to the chaplain, "Father, my rifle doesn't work." Father Vincent immediately took Sergeant Manfra's rifle and under fire ran to give the rifle to Rounseville. Again, Father Vincent returned to Manfra's side to give him comfort and minister to his wounds. Miraculously, Manfra would make a full recovery from his injuries. He owed his life to Father Vincent Capodanno.

As the battle continued, Father Vincent persisted in seeking out those in need, even in the midst of gunfire. He was wounded again during the late afternoon. Corporal Frederick W. Tancke, 2nd Platoon, described the chaplain's heroic perseverance and determination even after being hit a second time:

> He was then wounded by shrapnel in the arms, hand, and legs and refused medical attention. The corpsman tried to patch him together but he waved him off. He said he wanted the wounded Marines to be taken care of first.

Though Father Vincent could have left the battlefield at any time, he wanted to stay with his men, no matter what the cost. As Chaplain John Keeley, Division Chaplain, noted:

Chaplain Capodanno's action on that day symbolized an idea of the ministry to men in combat that transcended the immediacy of personal sacrifices and illuminated a concept of ministry which became unique to Vietnam, the ministry of adaptation that enabled the chaplain to be present as much as possible where needed.

Chaplain Eli Takesian simply and briefly summed up the reason for Father Vincent's heroic actions on the field of battle: "He just wanted to be with the Grunts. He was more a Marine than anything else. . . ."

Operation "Swift" continued throughout the day and early evening of September 4. Even though injured, Father Vincent tirelessly persisted in going from one wounded Marine to the next. He offered his comforting presence to all and the Sacrament of the Anointing of the Sick to Catholic Marines.

As the sun began to set at 6:30 p.m., the Marines of Company M, 2nd Platoon, were in a desperate situation. Their circle of defense was getting smaller and smaller as the enemy's attack became more intense; the need to rescue the wounded from the field and secure the perimeter became more urgent. According to official reports, these were the battle conditions in which Father Vincent performed his last heroic act.

Harton's Story

Perhaps Corporal Ray Harton provides the most powerful testimony of Father Capodanno's final minutes. Harton recounts:

> We were positioned at the base of a small knoll. Sgt. Peters came running up to us and said that the 1st Platoon had been hit hard on the other side of the knoll. We could hear the firing. He instructed me and two other Martines to follow him. As we topped the knoll and started down, Sgt. Pete was hit and was on the ground. The carnage started. He screamed at us, "Get that gun!" while pointing and firing at clump of bushes directly in front of us. I grabbed a grenade pouch as we leaped up to get closer to the gun. Two Marines next to me were killed; then a bullet tore into my left arm exiting through my elbow. Another bullet slammed into my rifle, rendering it useless. I screamed, "Corpsman, Corpsman," and tried to stop the bleeding. With every beat of my fast pumping heart though my

blood was pumping into the dirt. Every time I moved, that gun kept firing at me.

I don't know how long I lay there. I found myself getting weaker and could see the North Vietnamese soldiers moving in on us. They were close. I spotted our Corpsman, "Doc" Leal, moving my way under fire. He looked at me, and he was alone. I thought everyone else was dead. I prayed to God, for I knew I was bleeding to death, and the NVA were near. I expected a bullet or bayonet at any moment. As I closed my eyes, someone touched me. When I opened my eyes, he looked directly at me. it was Father Capodanno. Everything got still: no noise, no firing, no screaming. A peace came over me that is unexplainable to this day. In a quiet and calm voice, he cupped the back of my head and said, "Stay quiet, Marine. You will be OK. Someone will be here to help you soon. God is with us all this day." I noticed he had a lot of blood on his head and face. His right hand, covered with dirty and bloody bandages, was almost gone, so he blessed me with his left hand. I heard a scream close by, My leg, my leg!" I was jolted back to my senses. It was "Doc" Leal who was sitting holding his leg just a few feet from me. Father Capodanno leaped up and ran to "Doc." As he supported "Doc" Leal the machine gun that I was supposed to destroy opened up killing them both. As the first bullet from that gun entered the back of Father Capodanno's head, I knew I had failed in my mission. That was the last time I saw Father Capodanno, but it wasn't my first.

On Sunday, the day before, Father Capodanno had Mass at our Company Area. I can remember his voice and the way he always looked at us directly. His message seemed to be, "Keep the faith" or "God is with us" or words to that effect. When the Mass was over, he invited anyone to stay and talk.

A few weeks before then Father Capodanno appeared out of the darkness as we prepared for Operation Cochise. He sat and talked with us offering us goodies of cigarettes, candy, gum, fruit that were hidden in his big fatigue pockets. He had a poem that made us laugh about the Marines that he had found in the *Marine Corps Gazette*. He passed out a copy that I still have today.

"Marines are found everywhere: in barracks, in bars, in love, on leave and in debt. A Marine."

When things got tough, Father Capodanno always showed up.

I remember the first time I met him was in late July just after I arrived in Vietnam with the 5th Marines. We had just come off a patrol and were at the Chow Tent. A small group of Marines was in the corner of the tent laughing and talking. A man called us over to join them. It was Father Capodanno. I thought he was just another Marine, but in a few minutes I realized he was a chaplain, because of his calm voice, his praise for us and for the job we were doing, and his direct look. He was the same that first time I met him as he was the last time I met him.

Corporal Tancke was only a few yards away from Father Vincent when the priest was killed by enemy fire. He has provided another account of the event.

I was trying to stop the bleeding (of corpsman Armando G. Leal, who had been hit in the thigh and groin and was bleeding to death from a major artery), when I saw an enemy with a machine gun about 15 meters away. I was shot in the finger and dived into a hole to return fire [Tancke's M-16 jammed and he was not able to fire]. When Chaplain Capodanno got about 40 meters down the hill he stopped for a second. I said, 'Watch out, there's a Viet Cong with a machine gun.' The Viet Cong laughed at me, squatted down with his machine gun and stayed there. The Chaplain was crouched down in cover and seeing the corpsman, he jumped out from cover and ran over about 20 feet to the corpsman, right to his side. I heard enemy machine gun fire and the Chaplain fell by the corpsman's side. He actually jumped out in front of a machine gun that the North Vietnamese Army had about 15 meters from me and the wounded. He had begun to give medical attention to the corpsman and three or four wounded Marines when the machine gunner opened up and killed him. I am sure he knew the Viet Cong machine gunner was there and was set up. The Viet Cong fired two bursts, both of which hit near me, and one or both bursts hit the Chaplain. Two men near me grenaded the machine gun and destroyed it.

Both Father Vincent and Corpsman Leal were killed instantly by the blast of automatic fire. The chaplain and corpsman — the two noncombatants on the field — were killed together. The end came swiftly and mercilessly for Father Vincent; he received twenty-seven bullet wounds in his spine, neck, and head. The sacrifice and suffering which the young seminarian had studied in *Radiating Christ* a decade before, now was consummated.

Fourteen other Marines were killed and thirty-one were wounded in this single conflict. Removing the fallen from the field was not an easy task. PFC Julio Rodriguez was one of the men who tried to recover Father Vincent's fallen body. Rodriguez noted:

> Five of us went to get Father; three Marines were hit while trying to bring in his body. We had to leave him because of the intense fire which had pinned us down. That night we succeeded in bringing in Father's body. When we found him he had his right hand over his left breast pocket. It seemed as if he was holding his Bible. He had a smile on his face and his eyelids were closed as if asleep or in prayer.

Even while the battle raged on, the word of the revered chaplain's death spread like a blaze throughout the battalion. "The chaplain's hit, the chaplain's hit," was the message passed from platoon to platoon. Through radio transmission, official word of his death was received by the 5th Marine combat center. Major Alger, the Regimental Operatons Officer, was with Colonel Davis when Father Vincent's death was announced. They heard: "3/5, number twenty-one is KIA." Twenty-one is the numerical code for a chaplain. Both Alger and Davis refused to believe the report and asked the radio operator to repeat the message. All became silent in the normally busy and noisy combat center.

Chaplain Takesian, who was positioned with an element of 3/5 less than a half-mile from Father Vincent's body, noted that after his unit was informed of the death "everything became still. It was as if a shroud had covered the entire battalion." Marines, Grunts and officers alike, openly wept for their fallen chaplain. Corporal Tim Hanley, who was also near the battle scene, stated, "It was like playing chess and you lost your queen — morale-wise it was devastating." .

Corporal James Hamfeldt, a gunner in 1/5, heard about Father Vincent's death several days later. The news of his death had a profound and emotional effect on Hamfeldt:

> He gave his life. No one can do any more than that — that's what Christ did. . . . The only way I can justify it, is that he did it because that is what he had to do, and if he is going to be a priest and a Christian there really can't be any other way. I know that but it still kills me. . . . Of all the deaths I saw and did, the greatest was his. I don't know if he knew the tremendous impact he had on me. I came back to Church because of Father Capodanno. In my life he is a saint.

Chaplain John Kelley, the Division Chaplain, received news of Father Vincent's death early on the morning of September 5. Chaplain Lawrence Lowry, who was now stationed at the 1st Medical Battalion in Da Nang, but had previously replaced Father Vincent at the 7th Marines, received the painful news directly from wounded Marines coming from Operation "Swift." Lowry was the first to notify Chaplain Keeley. Keeley's notation of the announcement in his logbook reads:

> Telephone call at 1:45 AM. Fr. Vincent Capodanno is killed. Larry Lowry called. Confirmed by Colonel Sam Davis who encouraged him to move forward. Canceled trip to Chulai for inspection. 57 killed, over 100 wounded in same battle. Much consternation.

"Swift" continued for another ten days; many more lives were lost. Marine corpses were slowly taken from the field during intermittent periods of calm. Father Vincent's body was removed from the field and lined up with the rest of his slain comrades near the helicopter landing zone. Simple rain ponchos covered the faces of the dead waiting for helicopter space to transport them to the central Army mortuary in Da Nang. According to Takesian, Father Vincent's body was immediately flown back to Da Nang.

Within days of the priest's death, the whole Marine Corps in Vietnam seemed to mourn his loss. From the 5th Marines to the 7th, those who knew Father Vincent were in shock. Small memorial services in memory of Father Vincent Capodanno were held throughout the various commands by many of the chaplains.

Chaplain Keeley gave one of the first services at Hill 63, the command post of the 2nd Battalion, 5th Marines. In his homily at the Mass, he summed up the sentiments that would be echoed by many in the coming days:

Last Monday evening, the 4th of September, the FIRST Battalion, FIFTH Marines, ran into or came under attack from approximately six thousand North Vietnamese regulars. . . . [Capodanno] died as he had lived these past months: brave and impulsive, heroic and self-sacrificing. He would not have had it any other way. He could not have been talked out of it.

'Touch not my anointed,' we hear the good Lord say, 'and to my prophets do no harm.' And so I shall not touch Father Capodanno except to praise him. To his memory, no harm shall be done. . . . However, and this is the first point of this little talk . . . who is there among us here today who would not wish and pray that Father Capodanno could continue to walk among us, to spread his Christ-like charm and warmth of personality even further, to act like the magnet he was to draw the best out of each one of us? The second point is to question how you will protect this next vibrant, kind and sensitive priest whom I shall send you [so] that he can help and minister to many over many, many weeks, months, and even years.

. . . but we must face facts . . . Father 'was touched' . . . he is dead. He was harmed . . . his body now lies at Med Battalion waiting for transfer home. We know Father was not trained to fight . . . he was a man of God, of peace. He was not trained to protect himself on the field of battle. . . . That Father Capodanno died serving his Marines, being near to wounded and dying, inspiring all who were fortunate to have come under his influence . . . all this is good . . . but it is also ended.

Now the second question. What is to be done to preserve his successor? Certainly not that his successor is to be kept in a gilded cage, restricted, hamstrung from moving about. . . .

The Biggest question here today is: 'Do you love your chaplains, your priests, your ministers?' If the answer is to be given in the positive . . . then I have only one word to give you: 'Protect them, then, protect them even against themselves.' I pray you know what I mean.

The words of Chaplain Keeley urged the Marines of 2/5 as

well as all Marines to watch out for their chaplains. Father Vincent's zeal for souls did lead to his death; however, it was not Father Vincent's will to die. His only resolve was to do the will of God. He was compelled by Christian love and self-sacrifice. Throughout his service in Vietnam, Father Vincent showed nothing but dedicated devotion to his Grunts. While his death is a tragic reality, it is a true testimony to his whole life of service as a priest.

Other chaplains pointed to these same qualities in their memorial services. Chaplain Roy Baxter sought to explain Father Vincent's death:

> Colleagues have asked me, 'Do you think he had a martyr complex?' My answer is emphatically and unequivocally, No! Everything about him showed that he loved life. Above all, he was the bearer of the Good News of the One who said, 'I am come that they might have life, and that they might have it more abundantly.' (John 10:10) When the word was received by the command on the dire situation of the beleaguered platoon, I do not think Vince took the time for an introspection to determine what motives should govern his actions. It was a spontaneous response, not contemplative of the peril he would face. It was an act of love. . . . Anyone who knew Vince was well aware of his altruistic nature. His ministry was a gift of love. To me, he was missions-oriented — the greater the need, the greater the concern and focus of one's life.

Chaplain Joseph F. Cloonan, a Navy chaplain and priest serving in Vietnam, did not know his fallen colleague; yet, he was motivated to write a poetic and moving account of Father Vincent's sacrifice. Cloonan's sentiments were printed in several publications under the title "A Bell for Capodanno":

> 'Ask not for whom the bell tolls, it tolls for thee.'
>
> The mystical poet, Donne, wrote those words in a symbolic sense. No man, he said, was an island; each is part of the main. When any man dies, his death means some dying for everyone else.
>
> In a graphic sense, he was showing how we all are tied up with one another, by bonds of love and even at times by other less worthy bonds, such as hate, etc.

Last night — which will be three weeks from last night as you read this — I got word of the death of a priest whom I have heard of but never met.

But I have a deep feeling of personal loss.

For what I have heard of this dedicated priest sums up this way: He was a man who tried as hard as he could to share in the struggles and sufferings of the men to whom he ministered. He worked among men who were in the constant threat of death, and among them he died.

He died in the act of assisting the wounded, Marines wounded in one of the fiercest actions of the Vietnam conflict.

Did he die willingly? Who knows what is in another man's mind at the moment of death? Was he there willingly? Yes.

He had already served his stint there and had been granted permission to extend it for another six months. He had also asked for a second extension, but death denied that request.

Last week I talked with another priest who had been in Vietnam for a year. He talked of suffering and death and of how fear can sneak up on you and take you by surprise just when you think you have yourself well in hand.

He also talked about how tough it was just being here. . .in a hot, heavy, humid climate that you wore like an envelope of penance . . . with prickly heat, skin rash, irritating itches, and the constant clamoring of the body for the feel of cool, clean water.

A wise man once said that poverty was bearable but that the things that accompany poverty are not. For the poor man is often despised, ignored, abused, ridiculed. These are harder to take than the poverty. War is hell, but the accompaniments of war are more hellish.

If he knew that the result of his sufferings would be quick success, and more importantly — lasting success, it would be more bearable.

If he knew that the innocent and the helpless would be guaranteed protection after his help was withdrawn, his dying and, more costly, his living, might not seem to be in vain. . . .

But men like Father Capodanno, who knew the people and the whole area from his work as a missioner, know that there is no magic formula for success, no quick recipe for victory. . . .

I think that's why Father Capodanno stayed in Vietnam long after he could have been rotated home.

While less dedicated men yawn through monotonous days and nights and call them comfortable, he was uncomfortable in the knowledge of the terrible need of others who couldn't help themselves. He who as a missioner had extended his hand and his heart to those who didn't know God now, as a chaplain, extended his life among those who were fighting the cause of the helpless.

But every once in a while, like a flash of heat lightning, the self-giving of someone like Father Capodanno illuminates the mystery of nobility in an ignoble world.

Chaplain Keeley commented further about Lieutenant Capodanno's death in his official report:

There are some who would question Chaplain Capodanno's wisdom and prudence on the day he was killed; but none would question his integrity or sense of mission. . . . Chaplain Capodanno was compelled to be with his men according to the dictates of his conscience and an overwhelming desire to serve his 'grunts.' The priorities of ministry, as interpreted by him, did not allow another course of action. His conviction and dedication to a ministry practically applied cost him his life. . . . Chaplain Capodanno's ministry to his men on that day of crisis illuminated the very best attitude toward the chaplain's ministry. His was a ministry of love and personal concern, and his conduct on the field of battle was inspired by his belief that this type of service to man was temporally and eternally profitable. . . . All who knew this priest were familiar with the selflessness he had made the core of his ministry, a selflessness that was to promote the actions which placed his life in jeopardy. Under critical analysis the reasoning behind this kind of human behavior, behavior that led in Chaplain Capodano's instance to the giving up of his life, appears complex and not easily understood. But in the case of this sacrifice lies simplicity of purpose — Chaplain Capodanno knew where he had to be and why. Chaplain Eli Takesian, who knew Chaplain Capodanno well, had only this brief answer to explain Chaplain Capodanno's actions; it is perhaps the most deeply moving and eloquent tribute to that man of God. 'He just wanted to be with the grunts. He was more a Marine than anything else. . . .'

The formal memorial service for Father Vincent was held on September 13, 1967, at the 1st Marine Division Headquarters in Da Nang. While Father Vincent was with the 1st Battalion, 7th Marines he participated in a similar memorial service and offered these very fitting words about memorials and honors to those who have died:

> We are assembled to pay homage to men we knew and admired. . . . God loved them or they would not have been born. God called them when they were most prepared to go. Do not let their names become empty memories. Recall to mind all their good points, the many things we admired in them. Imitate them. In that way their lives will be perpetuated among us. Our monument to them will not be of bronze or marble, but the living monument of all the good we saw in them.

Chaplain Takesian was flown into Da Nang from the field of battle in order to deliver the eulogy. When Takesian arrived, he recalled that several officials immediately asked him to change from his worn and dirty uniform into a freshly pressed one. They also gave him polish to shine his bloodstained combat boots. In respect for the men who had died in "Swift," Takesian refused to cover the blood that spotted his boots.

The chaplain's first request was to drive over to the Army mortuary. He wanted to see and identify for himself Father Vincent's body. Takesian remembered that the mortuary was a long quonset hut structure containing uncountable "bloated, grotesque bodies, stinking of death." An Army Master Sergeant, a devout Roman Catholic, took Chaplain Takesian to Father Vincent's body. It was not bloated like the rest, but looked as if the priest were peacefully sleeping. According to Takesian, the Master Sergeant wept slightly as he said, "When I heard what Father had done for his boys, I personally prepared his body." Takesian further recalled:

> We counted 27 gunshot wounds . . . saw the shrapnel embedded in his shoulder . . . and some fingers missing from his hand. The shot that killed him entered his head from the back of his neck. Most of the gunshot wounds were in the back. Usually, we looked down upon anyone with a wound

in his back because it was a sign of running away ... in Capodanno's case, it verified what eyewitnesses had said. Capodanno, having seen an NVA machine gunner aim his weapon at a cluster of Marines, ran and deliberately shielded one of them with his own body, back turned to the NVA. Whether he was praying at the time is cloudy. Some said he was ... others said he wasn't. ... Whatever the case, his action was a profound prayer itself.

The Requiem Mass was held at the 1st Marine Division chapel. The chapel was jammed, especially by the 7th Marines who came by buses and trucks from Chu Lai in order to honor their former chaplain. The 5th Marines were still involved in Operation "Swift" and could not attend in large numbers. Chaplain Keeley was the celebrant for the Mass and Chaplain Henry Lavin offered the memorial prayers. Father Vincent's brother Philip also attended. At the time, Philip Capodanno worked as an engineer for Atlantic and Pacific Architects in Saigon.

Chaplain Takesian's eulogy mentioned Father Vincent's heroic deeds and compared his actions to those of Christ himself:

> Chaplain Vincent Robert Capodanno died in the manner in which he lived: unselfishly. He was ascetic, humble and thoughtful, a man imbued with the spirit of Christ. ...
>
> Later, upon hearing the fatal news, a young Marine came to me and tearfully asked, 'If life meant so much to Chaplain Capodanno, then why did he allow his own to be taken?' 'The answer is in your question,' I replied. 'It was precisely because he loved life — *the lives of others* — that he so freely gave his own.'
>
> Vincent Capodanno emptied himself; and his death has emptied us. Yet, paradoxically, we are filled, inspired, by his humility and courage. His was an act of grace, an emulation of Jesus Christ. ...
>
> His was the pilgrimage of a saint. Even to the end he faithfully held to the precept of our Lord that 'greater love hath no man than this, that a man lay down his life for his friends.'
>
> For the life and Christian witness of Chaplain Vincent Robert Capodanno, thanks be to God. Amen.

After the Mass, Takesian returned to the 3rd Battalion, 5th

Marines base camp. He and a Second Lieutenant went to Father Vincent's small tent and identified personal belongings for the next of kin. Takesian described entering Father Vincent's tent as an eerie experience:

> He had two neat groupings. Clothing and materials which belonged to the government; and his own personal effects. Usually, troops and others are kind of messy about such stuff . . . perhaps a way of denying the reality of death. The first thing that went through my mind was, 'Did Vinnie know he was going to die?' I don't know the answer to that. I do know he was prepared for any eventuality . . . continuing life or sudden death.

On September 15, 1967, Chaplain Charles T. Kelly reported for temporary duty as the Catholic chaplain for the 5th Marines. During the one month he served as chaplain, Kelly was instrumental in documenting many of the acts of Father Vincent's last few hours in the battle. Kelly noted in his final report that "following Father Vincent was like attending a class in what a good chaplain should do. He knew every man by name and all knew him."

Two weeks later, Chaplain John J. Lepore reported for duty as the permanent Catholic chaplain for the 5th Marines, replacing Chaplain Kelly. Lepore also was impressed by the accounts he heard of his predecessor.

The legacy that Father Vincent left his predecessors continues into our own time. Tertullian, an early Church historian, noted that the blood of martyrs is the seed of Faith. Father Vincent is a Christian martyr, not in the sense that he was killed *for* the Faith, but that his death was an act of love *because of* the intensity of his faith. He never stood idle in the face of human suffering; he was a man of action who always remained faithful to his Christian convictions and missionary vocation. His death was not futile, nor was his life forgotten. For the Christian, one who dies in an act of love never dies in vain. Jesus assured his disciples, "A grain of wheat remains no more than a single grain unless it is dropped into the ground and dies. If it does die, then it produces many grains." (Jn: 12:24-25) By the manner of his life and death, Father Vincent bore witness to his faith, so much so that his testimony continues now, reaching out beyond the small grassy knoll where his body fell, to all men and women of good will who seek closer union with God and a life of authentic love and service.

AN INSPIRATION:
Memorials to Father Vincent Capodanno

> *There is a thing more terrible than dying, and that
> is being buried; I mean being buried alive. To take
> part in the work of Redemption means following the
> Master even to that length.* Descendit; Incarnatus est;
> Passus; Sepultus est. *He came down from heaven, be-
> came incarnate, died and was buried.*
>
> Raoul Plus, S.J.,
> *Radiating Christ: An Appeal to Militant Catholics*

On most mornings an eerie mist rolls in from the Potomac
River and enshrouds the Vietnam Veterans Memorial in the
nation's capital. The huge granite wall stands as a massive yet
surprisingly graceful tribute to more than 58,000 men and
women who died a half a world away. Such a tribute was slow in
coming, but for seventeen years now, the Wall has been a beacon
for those who want to remember loved ones in a country that
yearns to forget the war in which they fought and died. Emotions
run high at the Wall, and so they should: young men and women,
full of promise, are missed by millions even now, a generation
after their deaths. Each name etched on the 492-foot monument
tells a story of life, love and death. In some cases, it is a narrative
of quiet sacrifice, while in others it may be one of pain and suffering. Each of these names is an inspiration to a society which
often seems unwilling to acknowledge the value of honor, responsibility and commitment.

During the sixties and early seventies, homes across this land
were touched by these deaths. It has often been said that death is

a great equalizer, and no more so than in war. No family member with a loved one in Vietnam could rest easily knowing — fearing — that an unwelcome knock on the front door might come at any time.

Throughout the nation on September 5, 1967, military officials fanned out to inform 127 families that a son or husband had been killed in Operation "Swift." On Staten Island, James Capodanno's home on Seacrest Boulevard was one of those visited. The fear that had gripped him as he watched the news the night before was now a reality: his youngest brother was dead.

While a feeling of numbness and disbelief descended on the whole Capodanno family, the world quickly learned of their little brother's death. That Tuesday, September 5, many newspapers carried the news of Chaplain Vincent Capodanno's heroic sacrifice. From the *New York Times* to the *Stars and Stripes*, the headlines told the story: "Chaplain Killed in Battle While Helping His 'Grunts,'" "Chaplain's Epitaph: He Was a Marine," and "Chaplain From S.I. [Staten Island] Killed Praying on Battlefield." As the word continued to spread, the Capodanno family received calls and letters of condolence from friends, officials in the government and the military, Maryknoll priests and sisters, chaplains, and those who were simply moved by the story.

Messages arrived from President Lyndon B. Johnson, Secretary of the Navy Paul R. Ignatius and Mayor John V. Lindsay of New York. Robert Kennedy, New York's junior senator, sent a letter of condolence to the family that read, in part:

> I was grieved to learn of the death of your brother. Winston Churchill said, 'Courage is rightly esteemed as the first of all human qualities because it is the one that guarantees all others.' This courage Lieutenant Capodanno gave to all of us. To him and to his family are due the thanks of a humbly grateful nation.

Two Maryknoll priests, Father Don Sheehan, himself an Air Force chaplain, and Father John Shields, expressed the heartfelt loss of Father Vincent to the Society, to them personally, and the great influence Capodanno had had on many. Father Sheehan wrote:

> I can gauge somewhat the keen sorrow that must be yours and your family's, for I too feel as if I had lost a brother. And

yet, Pauline, I so felt like starting this note out — "Congratulations" — because I think that that is the way Vinnie would look at it.

When news of your mother's death reached Vinnie, I was with him. And I still recall vividly the words he spoke after the funeral Mass he celebrated for her in Maioli. He remarked to his Chinese audience how wonderful it was that so many people, whom your mother never met or knew, were praying for her then. And now, I can't help but think of how that applies to Vinnie himself. Only God knows how many lives he has touched in his priestly ministry — in the States, on Taiwan, and lastly in Vietnam.

The words of the Preface of the Mass — 'Life is not taken away, but only changed' — these words have to be our consolation, Pauline. We could grieve at our loss, of not seeing Vinnie again in this world — but I guess we really should rejoice that Vinnie has attained his goal — eternal life.

It is my prayer that God will grant you peace of heart, in knowing that it was love that killed Vinnie — not any bullet — but a Christ-like love, and that love was the greatest known to man, that it brought him to lay down his life as he did.

Father Shields wrote to fellow Maryknoller Father Dick Murto about the amazing effect the story of Father Vincent's death had on one young woman:

When Vinnie Capodanno died I told the story of his life to one of my English groups in a local company. One young woman, Miss Makiko Furumura, a filing clerk, about 25 years old, was very struck, and seemingly touched to the heart. There evidently was something going on in her heart, and Vinnie's generosity inspired her to no end. She told me the same, gave me money for flowers for [the]church (she's [an] anonymous Christian . . . no religion) and also gave me about two bucks to send to Vinnie's mother. . . .

Two weeks ago the girl appeared with a box of 1000 cranes. She had slaved every off-working hour for over a month to make them. With each crane, a hand-made thing, she made a request for Vinnie's peace and happiness, his family's well-being. To what God I know not. I only know she loved Vinnie for what he did and has experienced [sic] new life from her concern for him and his family. . . .

Isn't it strange how our lives have a message for people and in ways we'd never guess. Vinnie's has had this for so many. . . .

Sister Maria Consuela, a Maryknoll Sister who knew Father Vincent in the missions, also wrote to the family. She stressed his great example of priestly character and his true witness to the Christian belief of eternal life:

My memory of Father is and always will be of one of the finest most priestly of priests. In the world today, many priests turn from the beautiful vocation God has called them to but Father Capodanno could find his fulfillment only in being a *priest*, a holy and dedicated priest. It is difficult to understand why God wanted Father in Vietnam now, his sojourn in Taiwan was like a stepping-stone into more difficult areas, but there were souls there, in need and I'm sure Father will meet them in heaven.

Colleagues in the field who knew Father Vincent wrote to the family trying to comfort them with the details of his life and the great effect he had on so many. Chaplains Thomas J. Woolten, J. D. Shannon and John J. O'Connor offered their thoughts on a fallen friend. Chaplain Woolten wrote:

I know and swear that there are living chapels in Vince's name. 'Those grunts' saw Christ when they saw Vince. This may appear like pious rhetoric but I have been a priest too long not to comprehend how people react when sentences are used to tell people the happening of an event. When 'these grunts' learned of Vince's death, it was pathetic to watch their reactions. A lump came to my throat, Pauline, and I know I'm a tough man emotionally.

Chaplain Shannon, who knew Vincent Capodanno since chaplain school in Newport, noted, "It was apparent from the beginning that Vince would make a good chaplain. He was intense, yet friendly; devoted to his calling; and earnest in his dealing with everyone."

Chaplain John J. O'Connor, who would one day become Cardinal Archbishop of New York and Chief of Chaplains for the Navy, wrote to Mrs. Pauline Costa noting the great respect other chaplains had for her brother:

I am sure you would like to know that very recently I made a trip to Vietnam and talked with a number of men who had lived and worked with Vince. I never heard a priest praised more consistently. One of his greatest admirers, as you probably know, was an Episcopal Chaplain — Chaplain Krulak. I talked at length with Chaplain Krulak, and he confirmed my impressions — that in the manner of his death, just as in the way he lived, Vince inspired men as few others have done.

I served in Vietnam in 1965, before Father Vince arrived, and know the terrain, the problems, the nature of the conflict in which he found himself. I know well the area in which he died, and when I was in this general vicinity on the occasion of my recent visit, I offered Mass for him.

This was a heroic priest in life and in death. I have no doubt that he is enjoying the reward of that heroism at this moment.

The Capodannos received many letters from strangers around the world who were touched by their brother in some way. Many of the people who wrote knew him only slightly or for a short period of time. Still, his effect on their lives was just as substantial as those who had known him for years. Mrs. Lola L. Wilder and Mr. Thomas C. Panian were just two of the many who testified to his enduring memory. In a long letter to the family, Mrs. Wilder wrote:

It was a great honor to meet your brother, Chaplain Capodanno. Our meeting was one of 'chance,' a once in a lifetime thing. I'll never forget the impression he made on me, his true devotion, truly a man of God. I marveled at his desire to be back over there helping. . . .

He talked of his being home and what he'd done and how he enjoyed it, but of how useless and out of place he'd felt in the states and of his great desire to return to his work amongst the fighting and the boys where he was needed. He said he didn't know what he'd do when this six months extension was up as he felt that was where he would do most good. . . .

He did seem very happy and talked as if he was doing just as his heart desired. Our conversation went on for a long time, he said he was in no hurry and enjoying it.

I felt such comfort and peace of mind talking to him and thought how wonderful he must be with the boys over there. I feel I'll live the rest of my days and never meet anyone like him again. His image and kindness will be in my memory as long as I live. . . .

I felt so lost, shocked and grief stricken. I knew him for only about an hour and a half and yet feel as if I've lost a lifetime friend. God was good to share him with me for even so brief a time.

Mr. Thomas Panian also wrote of the time he spent with Father Vincent. Although the relationship was short, Panian's memories of this priest, and especially of his convictions regarding death, would last a lifetime:

He wasn't someone you would talk to; he was someone who could listen to you. No matter what problems, apprehensions or fears one of us might have had he understood just what troubled us. . . . We knew how he felt about death. Like every man he wanted to live but unlike every man he was unafraid to die. His duty to God, service and his Marines overshadowed any personal fear. No, we were sorry for ourselves mostly. Sorry that we'd lost the man who gave us counsel and fortitude whenever and wherever we needed it.

The words that many wrote helped to allay the pain for the family and helped tell a more complete story of Father Vincent's deeds. His valiant death was only the mirror of his heroic life. The testimonies of those who knew Father Vincent continued to flesh out the man, the priest and the military chaplain.

Philip Capodanno accompanied the mortal remains of his brother home to Staten Island. Just ten days after the fatal events in Operation "Swift," the body of the fallen chaplain landed in California. Following the path of all military personnel who died in Vietnam, the casket was then flown to Dover Air Force Base in Delaware. Finally, on Friday, September 16th, a train carried Vincent Capodanno home to Staten Island. His sister Pauline requested that the closed casket be brought to her home in Kearny, New Jersey, where a wake was held the following weekend.

Countless people came to visit during these days of mourning. For the first time, the family realized what an incredible affect their brother had on the lives of so many people. Many of the chaplains and field officers who had known Father Vincent in

Vietnam made the pilgrimage to New Jersey for the wake and the funeral. From Father Vincent's first assignment with the 7th Marines, Major Ed Fitzgerald, and Captains Jerry Pendas and Chuck Brookfield attended the funeral.

On September 18, the casket was taken to Queen of Peace Church in North Arlington, New Jersey, where the body lay in state through the night. It was at Queen of Peace, just a short distance from Pauline's home, that Father Vincent often celebrated Mass when he was home on leave from the missions or the military. At 11:00 a.m. the next morning, the Requiem Mass was said.

Queen of Peace Church was filled to overflowing. The Maryknoll choir sang for the Mass, and a military honor guard carrying the colors escorted the casket to the sanctuary of the church. The Chief of Chaplains, Rear Admiral James W. Kelly, was present along with nearly eighty-five chaplains of all denominations and from all branches of the service. Cardinal Spellman also attended; it was only nine and a half years since he had ordained Father Vincent at Ossining.

Among other religious dignitaries present were Archbishop Thomas A. Boland of the Newark Diocese, and Bishop William J. Moran of the Military Ordinariate. Father John J. McCormack, Superior General of Maryknoll, and Bishop John M. Comber, former Superior of the Society and the one who gave Father Vincent permission to join the Chaplain Corps, were also concelebrants of the Mass. The pastor of Queen of Peace, Monsignor LeRoy E. McWilliams, and about forty-seven Maryknoll priests were in the procession. All had come to pay one last tribute to a fellow classmate, priest, or chaplain.

Father Eugene F. Higgins of Maryknoll gave a stirring and challenging eulogy paralleling Vincent Capodanno's life with the life of Christ. Father Higgins spoke of how Father Vincent had grown in the spiritual life and had become a holier person because he truly sought to radiate Christ:

> And yet how profound must be your joy at this moment. That a member of your own family should be God's instrument as the inspiration for many young men throughout this country is no small honor. The Liturgy of the Mass with its

white vestments for the concelebrants symbolize the sorrow
and the joy that we all feel with you today — they symbolize
the death and resurrection of Father Vince with Christ.

. . .Today, September 19 — the day of his burial — you
and I have the privilege together with this proud Capodanno
family — to pay our tribute to Vincent Capodanno — Christian — priest — missionary — Marine Chaplain — American.

A twenty-year-old corporal said of Father Vince, 'Somehow he just seemed to act the way a man of God should act.'
How true this is! But to know anything about human spiritual
growth is to know that all growth takes place over a long period of time. That mature man sometimes is chosen to epito-
mize his whole life of love and dedication in one heroic action.
This is Father Capodanno's story. . . . My recollections give
witness to how truly he grew over the years so that his dedication on that dusty battlefield at Tamky, South Vietnam on September 4th was no accident. His whole life was a preparation as
one report mentioned, 'to keep going from wounded to
wounded and from dead to dead. The very last time he was
seen alive, he was saying a prayer over a dead man.'

For any Christian to grow — be he layman or priest — he
must grow in Christ. Jesus Christ — the Word — the expression of God who became a human being and lives among us
— a man who has compassion and mercy on his fellow man
because he is one of us — who knows the pain of the body and
the loneliness of the human heart — who could laugh over the
joys of life and smile at the antics of little children. He cried
when his dear friend died and wept over a city that did not recognize him — he became violently angry over injustices and
superficialities. . . .

Then to solidify his whole life of his love for his friends
— his service to mankind and his message of peace, Jesus allowed his life to be taken that through death new life might
blossom forth, 'for greater love has no man than he give up his
life for his friend.'

As we have attempted to briefly summarize the life of
Jesus, there is not one person here today who cannot recognize
from where Father Capodanno's strength and love and dedication came. Firstly, he was a full human being who could laugh
and cry — who became angry over the injustices that exist in
this world. . . . He felt very much at home talking with a

Formosan farmer in his poor brick hut over a simple Chinese meal or dropping in unexpectedly in a tent to sip beer with the enlisted men in the battle zone.

And so we have gathered here today to be part of Father Capodanno's last earthly celebration. We are all sad this moment over the loss of a dear friend, but Father Capodanno himself is enjoying the company of his parents and all who have learned life's purpose here on earth and have departed for the joys that are reserved for those who have loved God. One skeptic on hearing about the death of Father Capodanno mentioned how foolish he was not to take better precaution regarding his safety. How shallow this skeptic. He could not realize that only a man who truly loves his life could expose it to death in the service of another. 'The seed must fall to the ground in order to bring forth new life.' Let us pray that the death of Christ — the deaths of a Doctor Dooley in the service of mankind — of President Kennedy in the service of his country — or a Father Capodanno will not bespeak foolishness, but will spark new life in each who is familiar with his sacrifice.

No more tears now for Father Capodanno who by his life realized in what true greatness consists. Tears only for us who refuse to redirect our lives by the example of this young man's bravery in life and death 'for having loved those who were his own in this world he loved them to the very end.'

After the Requiem Mass, the casket was taken in procession to its final place of rest. James Capodanno remembered that many lined the procession route. One of the parishes along the way, Blessed Sacrament Church, honored Father Vincent by having all the doors of the church wide open and the bells ringing as the school children of the parish stood at attention along the road.

Father Vincent's body was interred at Saint Peter's, a small cemetery in the middle of a suburb on Staten Island where his mother and father are also buried. Maryknoll desired to have the body interred at the Society's cemetery in Ossining, New York, and the military asked that the burial take place at Arlington National Cemetery in Virginia; however, the family's desire was respected. At the gravesite, Bishop Comber performed the final commendation.

The ultimate level in the spiritual life of a Christian, as described by the book *Radiating Christ*, is the burial. As has been seen, Father Vincent clearly sought to be a dedicated priest — another Christ. In his last human act, he imitated the life and death of Christ in an immediate and dramatic way. As Saint Paul proclaims: "It is not I who live, but Christ who lives in me." (Galatians 2:19b-20). In an analogous way, Christ was buried deep within Father Vincent's heart and soul, and because Christ was buried in his soul, Father Vincent was able to die to himself and live only for Christ. This radical witness to Christ was ultimately the cause of Father Vincent's physical death. As Father Plus wrote in *Radiating Christ*:

> How discreet is this buried God within us! It would seem that He fears to frighten us by too manifest a presence, that he fears to impose Himself upon our wills in such a way as to diminish the freedom of our consent. So delicate, so discreet is His action that when, afterwards, we try to point to the exact moment in which that divine action began we often find it impossible to do so. It is the triumph of the imperceptible.

The lesson of all this is clear enough: in order to act upon our souls God buries Himself.

AN INSPIRATION:
MEMORIALS TO FATHER VINCENT CAPODANNO

The tributes to Father Vincent, which began shortly after his death, continue to call attention to his life thirty years later. These honors took many forms: chapels, military citations, a Navy ship, renamed streets, art work, and even a sculpture in his honor in the town square of Gaeta, Italy. The reason for the diversity is perhaps one of the most intriguing aspects of the life of Vincent Capodanno: he was a member of many brotherhoods. He was a priest, a Maryknoller, a Navy chaplain and an "honorary" Marine. He also was a member of a large, loving family. He affected each of these groups, and they affected him. Each has sought to honor his memory as a brother, friend and respected colleague.

THE CHAPELS

A memorial chapel is a fitting tribute for a chaplain: it is a place of prayer and peace, a safe haven from the troubles of the world, a place to speak with God. Father Vincent was, in his person, all of these things and more to the Marines he served. In a sense, he was a living chapel of hope. At least seven chapels have been dedicated to the memory of Father Vincent.

Fittingly, the first known chapel honoring him was the last chapel he helped build in Vietnam. Major Ed B. Burrow, 1st Battalion, 5th Marines, recalled dedicating 1/5's chapel shortly after Father Vincent was killed. The simple chapel was built on Hill 51 in the Que Son Valley and was constructed of thatched palms and bamboo with no walls. It served as a reminder to the Marines that their beloved chaplain was not forgotten.

Four months after Father Vincent's death, the first U.S. memorial to honor him was announced. A letter was sent to Pauline Costa from Chaplain Paul C. Hammerl of the Navy Chaplains School in Newport, Rhode Island, declaring the school's desire to dedicate the chapel there to the memory of Father Vincent. The Capodanno family immediately approved and made plans to attend the dedication.

The dedication took place on the first floor of building 117, the Chaplains School, at the Newport Naval Base on February 5, 1968. About 100 people, including twenty family members, attended the half-hour dedication ceremony. During the ceremony Pauline Costa unveiled a plaque in the back of the small chapel:

CAPODANNO MEMORIAL CHAPEL
DEDICATED TO THE MEMORY OF
CHAPLAIN VINCENT R. CAPODANNO, USNR
A MEMBER OF CLASS 1-66
U.S. NAVAL CHAPLAINS SCHOOL
24 SEPTEMBER 1966[2]*
KILLED IN ACTION IN VIETNAM, WHILE
MINISTERING TO THE WOUNDED MARINES OF
THE THIRD BATALLION [sic], FIFTH MARINES
4 SEPTEMBER 1967*

[2] The first date that appears on the plaque is incorrect; it should read 24 February 1966.

Also during the short ceremony, remarks were made by both Chaplain David Casazza, former Division Chaplain in Vietnam, and Chaplain James Kelly, Chief of Chaplains. Chaplain Casazza spoke personally of his experience with Father Vincent:

At Father Capodanno's funeral, I assisted my own Ordinary, Archbishop Boland, the Archbishop of Newark. During the procession into the church, the Archbishop asked me if I knew Father Capodanno in Vietnam. I said, 'Yes, Your Excellency, he was one of my chaplains. In fact, I assigned him to the unit in which he was killed.' 'Then,' he said slowly, 'You had a part in his death.' So, I did. But, I also had a part in his life — and he had a part in mine. One couldn't help but be affected by this man, this priest of God. He affected everyone who knew him.

As Christians and especially as clergymen, we all have our own picture of Christ. I guess our idea of what Christ is like varies from individual to individual. To me, this priest chaplain fitted my idea of Christ more than any other man I have ever met. He was strong; he was silent; he was a searcher. He was a quiet man with quick eyes. He spoke little but his presence was felt instantaneously. All of us usually fit into a mold of some sort. This man made his own mold. And every man who met him knew it. This man was different.

He was a hungry man — Hungry to be with his troops — Hungry for more time, more time to seek out the lonely Marine, more time to sit with the scared boy, more time to explain things to the confused platoon leader.

Chaplain Kelly spoke on the importance of memorials, that these man-made structures are our way of remembering those who have gone before and made such an impact on our lives, lest they be forgotten. Kelly commented:

Man has always set a high premium on his memorials. At the close of some very useful, heroic and sacrificial life we attempt an expression of appreciation by erecting a costly monument, naming something of importance after the hero or engaging in periodic ceremonies to keep his memory fresh in the minds of men.

. . .And now we borrow the name of Vincent Robert Capodanno to identify this chapel.

. . .By his superlative strength of purpose, determination,

and selfless and complete dedication, he has earned the right to live in our memory. And when men enter this chapel to pray, to meditate or to worship, they will sense not only the presence of the eternal God who calls them into a *Service of Love*, they will sense as well the influence of one who taught us all about the *Love of Service*.

In early 1979, the Chaplains School was moved from building 117 to building 114. The Father Capodanno Memorial Chapel was transferred at the same time. Today, all Navy chaplains continue to begin their Navy careers and training at Newport. For most of these chaplains, the name and the stories of Father Vincent are first heard at the place where Father Vincent himself fulfilled his first assignment.

The military continued to name chapels as a tribute to Father Vincent. On November 27, 1968, the Naval Hospital in Oakland, California, dedicated a chapel to his memory. The chapel on the Marine Corps Air Station in Iwakuni, Japan, also bears his name. The fifth chapel to be established in Father Vincent's honor is the Camp Margarita Chapel at Camp Pendleton, headquarters of the 5th Marines. On March 23, 1988, Chaplain Victor Krulak and James Capodanno took part in the dedication ceremony.

The sixth chapel to honor Father Vincent was sponsored by his family and Maryknoll, and located in Taiwan. This was the memorial the family decided to build in honor of their brother. They wanted a chapel built in Taiwan where none existed and where one was needed. A month after Father Vincent's death, the family wrote to Father Maynard Murphy in Taiwan concerning the erection of such a memorial. Father Murphy responded:

> Your letter was interesting, too, in that you mention a chapel for Vince. Vince always regretted there was no adequate or decent chapel in the City of Maioli where he was stationed for at least two years. . . . I'm sure Maryknoll would be quite interested in a chapel for Maioli City.

As early as December of 1967, Father William A. Bergan, Vicar General of Maryknoll, wrote to the family to inform them that $3,885 had already been received for the memorial chapel. The money was raised by many organizations such as the American Legion, Veterans of Foreign Wars, Knights of Columbus and the Marine Corps League. The goal of the Reverend Vincent Capodanno Memorial Fund committee was to raise $30,000. The chairman of the committee, Donald R. Marshall, wrote:

> Father Capodanno was the type of individual that always completed what he had started. It was his life desire to build a chapel in Taiwan and we of the committee would like to help fulfill his ambitions.

According to a letter sent by Bishop Frederick A. Donaghy, Father Vincent's former superior in Taiwan, to Father Bergan, the complete cost of the chapel would be only $6,000. In April 1970, Bishop Donaghy detailed the plans of the chapel:

> At the request of Father Jim Manning I am sending along some snapshots of St. Anne's Parish in the So. Miaoli, the mother mission of this Deanery. The house and property were purchased in the early 50s by Father Hilbert, in charge of the work here at that time. The house was converted to a chapel and residence and over the years has proved inadequate for either purpose; built on low ground dampness is a constant problem and on occasions heavy rains cause both the house and chapel to flood to the extent of two or three inches.
>
> It is on this site that we wish to construct the Capodanno Memorial Chapel should this project materialize. We feel it would prove to be a fitting memorial for Father Capodanno, who formerly worked here in Miaoli City, and it would also provide a fitting, and sorely needed, place of worship.

Ultimately, a chapel was built; however, not until the early nineties and not in the city of Maioli. Various factors contributed to putting the project on hold. In the late sixties when the money was sent to build the chapel, churches were not needed as they were in the fifties; furthermore, only $4,051 had been donated for the proposed chapel — not enough to begin the project. Two decades after planning the chapel, the cost to build rose significantly.

In 1987, Father Daniel Dolan, a Maryknoller and former pastor of Father Vincent's parish in Ta Hu, decided to build a chapel in the mountain town of Thiankou in the Ta Hu parish. Father

Dolan raised the rest of the money to complete the $82,000 chapel. The county government held up the construction of the chapel for a number of years until construction was finally begun in the Spring of 1993.

Also in the nineties, the Chapel at Fort Wadsworth on Staten Island was renamed for Father Capodanno. This brings the total number of such religious memorials to seven — and perhaps more will be dedicated in the new century.

THE MEDAL OF HONOR

The Medal of Honor is the highest military award which this nation can present. Since its inception in 1861 at the beginning of the Civil War, 3,410 Americans have received 3,429 medals; nineteen men were decorated twice. A universal reverence is accorded to those who have merited this honor. And so it should. The Medal of Honor is given "for a display of the most conspicuous gallantry and intrepidness above and beyond the call of duty — in the presence of an armed enemy. There must be a clear risk of life." The "Pyramid of Honor," as the Medal is called, was presented to 240 men who served in the Vietnam War. Of those, three were chaplains and Catholic priests; all of them earned their medals in a two-month period in the fall of 1967. They were two army officers, Major Charles J. Watters and Captain Charles J. Liteky, and Lieutenant Vincent R. Capodanno of the U.S. Navy.

On December 27, 1968, Secretary of the Navy Paul R. Ignatius told the Capodanno family that Father Vincent would receive the Medal of Honor. The relatives made plans to attend the ceremony along with many who had known him in Vietnam, including Major Ed Fitzgerald, Captain Jerry Pendas, and Chaplains Victor Krulak and Lawrence Lowry. The Medal of Honor ceremony was held at the Washington Navy Yard Sail Loft at 10:30 a.m., Tuesday, January 7, 1969.

The immediate Capodanno family, consisting of three brothers and five sisters and their families, arrived by train at Union Station in Washington, D.C., on the afternoon of January 6, 1969. All were escorted to the Shoreham Hotel for the night. On

January 7, the day of the presentation of the Medal of Honor, James Capodanno was chosen to receive the Medal. The official party to present the Medal and represent the United States, the Navy, and the Navy Chaplain Corps were Secretary Ignatius; Admiral Thomas H. Moorer, Chief of Naval Operations; Rear Admiral James W. Kelly, Chief of Chaplains; and Rear Admiral Donald G. Irvine, Commandant, Naval District, Washington. After the National Anthem, Ignatius made a few short remarks, and Admiral Moorer read the citation.

At the conclusion of the brief ceremony, Ignatius presented the Medal to a teary-eyed James Capodanno. In an expression of appreciation, the family gave the Navy Memorial Museum a commissioned oil painting of Father Vincent. The picture depicts him in his clerical suit, and in the background is a rendering of the last moments of his life.

Immediately after the ceremony, a memorial Mass was celebrated in memory of Father Vincent. The principal celebrant was Bishop William J. Moran, Military Vicar, and the priests concelebrating included Chaplains David J. Casazza and John J. O'Connor. Father John J. McCormack, Superior of Maryknoll, also was present. Approximately ninety Navy Chaplains, who came from as far away as California, participated in the Mass.

Father Vincent was honored as a true hero of Operation "Swift"; however, he was not the only one who received the Medal during that operation. He died a hero among many. Both Sergeant Rodney M. Davis, Company B, 1/5, and Sergeant Lawrence D. Peters, Company M, 3/5, were also posthumously awarded the Medal for their conspicuous gallantry and courage. Sergeant Peters received the Last Rites from Father Vincent before he died.

Lieutenant Capodanno became the 65th Vietnam serviceman and only the second Navy Chaplain to be awarded the Medal of Honor.

In addition to receiving the United States' highest military honor, Father Vincent also posthumously received the Purple Heart Medal.

It is evident from Father Vincent's own actions that he did

not pursue these military honors. His family was unaware that he had received the Vietnamese Cross of Gallantry with Silver Star and the Navy Bronze Star for his meritorious service during his six combat operations. Though he was notified of the Bronze Star, he did not seek to receive it in any kind of ceremony. Thirty-two years after his death, his brother James Capodanno officially accepted the medal for him on September 25, 1999.

The Congress takes pride in presenting the MEDAL OF HONOR posthumously to:

LIEUTENANT VINCENT R. CAPODANNO

CHAPLAIN CORPS

UNITED STATES NAVAL RESERVE

for service as set forth in the following

CITATION:

For conspicuous gallantry and intrepidity at the risk of his life above and beyond the call of duty as Chaplain of the 3rd Battalion, 5th Marines, 1st Marine Division (Rein), FMF, in connection with operations against enemy forces in Quang Tin Province, Republic of Vietnam on 4 September 1967. In response to reports that the 2nd Platoon of M Company was in danger of being overrun by a massed enemy assaulting force, Lieutenant Capodanno left the relative safety of the Company Command Post and ran through an open area raked with fire, directly to the beleaguered platoon. Disregarding the intense enemy small-arms, automatic-weapons, and mortar fire, he moved about the battlefield administering last rites to the dying and giving medical aid to the wounded. When an exploding mortar round inflicted painful multiple wounds to his arms and legs, and severed a portion of his right hand, he steadfastly refused all medical aid. Instead, he directed the corpsmen to help their wounded comrades and, with calm vigor, continued to move about the battlefield as he provided encouragement by voice and example to the valiant Marines. Upon encountering a wounded corpsman in the direct line of fire of an enemy machine gunner positioned approximately fifteen yards away, Lieutenant Capodanno rushed forward in a daring attempt to aid and assist the mortally wounded corpsman. At that instant, only inches from his goal, he was struck down by a burst of machine-gun fire. By his heroic conduct on the battlefield, and his inspiring example, Lieutenant Capodanno upheld the finest traditions of the United States Naval Service. He gallantly gave his life in the cause of freedom.

THE USS CAPODANNO

In the history of the United States Navy, seven ships have been named in memory of chaplains. The first was the *USS Livermore* (DD-429) named for Chaplain Samuel Livermore who distinguished himself on June 1, 1813, while aboard the *USS Chesapeake*. During an engagement with the British Navy, Livermore was wounded, thus becoming the first Navy Chaplain to be injured in combat. The *USS Livermore* was commissioned in 1940 and decommissioned sixteen years later.

Five World War II chaplains also were honored with ships named for them between 1968 and 1994. Chaplains O'Callahan, Schmitt, Kirkpatrick, Rentz and Laboon had all exemplified the highest form of sacrifice. Father Vincent Capodanno became a member of this elite brotherhood of chaplains.

On December 29, 1971, Vice Admiral Edwin B. Hooper, Director of Naval History, informed the Capodanno family that the Escort Ship DE-1093 would bear the name of Father Vincent Capodanno. Vice Admiral Hooper also informed Monsignor John McCormack, Superior General of Maryknoll, about the Navy's decision to name a ship after one of Maryknoll's own.

While the family received the news of this prestigious honor with delight, some in the Maryknoll Society were not so enthusiastic. Their apprehension demonstrated the effect of the Vietnam War on the United States. In February 1972, seventy-three priests, brothers, and seminarians of the Society signed a letter sent to Monsignor McCormack stating their concerns about a warship being named after Father Capodanno:

> We the undersigned desire to express our pleasure with the honor and esteem shown by the United States Navy for the courage and dedication of Father Vincent Capodanno. . . . Yet

we question the type of memorial proposed in his memory. We do not feel that the dedication of a warship . . . is a fitting tribute to a man who dedicated his life to bringing the peace and the love of Christ to others. . . .

Such a memorial is hardly in keeping with either the life and heroism of chaplains, in general, or the goals and aims of the Society of which this particular Chaplain was a member. Furthermore, the publicity surrounding the launching of such a ship would, we believe, disturb and sadden a large segment of the American people on whom this Society depends for support.

The group did suggest that another memorial be named after Father Capodanno instead of this symbol of war.

Monsignor McCormack responded to the "protest" letter, and stated:

I appreciate your expression to me of your personal views regarding what you considered the inappropriateness of naming a destroyer escort in memory of Father Capodanno. I have received other personal views from Maryknollers, who were highly elated upon hearing of the Navy's decision so to honor Father Capodanno.

Of course, it was only natural and appropriate and to be expected, that the members of Father Capodanno's immediate family, to whom the family name belongs, while still bereaved at the loss of their brother under such tragic circumstances, are extremely happy and proud and pleased with the fact that this vessel will bear his name.

While there were other letters received concerning the appropriateness of naming a warship after Father Vincent, Maryknoll did nothing officially to interfere with the event.

Avondale Shipyards in New Orleans built the vessel as one of a succession of twenty-seven single-purpose destroyer escorts in the Knox-class series. The main mission of the ship was to locate and destroy submarines. The keel of the ship, a landmark step in its construction, was laid on February 25, 1972.

On October 21, 1972, the destroyer escort was ready to be christened and launched. Many of the members of the Capodanno family were on hand in New Orleans for this historic event. The principal speaker at the ceremony was Chaplain Victor Krulak, who worked side by side with Father Vincent at the 1st Medical Battalion Hospital in Chu Lai. Mrs. William L. Springer, the wife of former Illinois Congressman Springer, was given the honor of christening the ship with a traditional bottle of champagne. After the crack of the bottle against its side, the ship was side-launched into the Mississippi River north of New Orleans.

On November 17, 1973, the *USS Capodanno* was commissioned at the Mayport Naval Station in Florida which then became the home port of the ship. Sixteen members of the family were present for the hour-long event. The first captain of the ship was Commander George W. Horsley, Jr., who assumed command during the commissioning ceremony. The tradition of commissioning a ship is a venerable ritual in which a pennant is raised above the ship for the first time. The long narrow pennant had seven stars in the union and horizontal red and white stripes at the point. The motto of the ship, "Duty with Honor," emphasized Father Vincent's role as both priest and military officer.

The principal speaker at the event was Congressman John M. Murphy, who represented New York's 17th district, including Staten Island. Murphy, a veteran Army officer from both World War II and the Korean War, spoke on the need for a strong military, but a military that also has compassion such as was shown by Father Vincent. During World War II, Murphy was a bunkmate at Fort Dix with PFC Joseph V. Merrill, a native of Staten Island who was also posthumously awarded the Congressional Medal of Honor, the only other Staten Islander beside Vincent Capodanno to be so honored. Ironically, Merrill also had a ship named after him: one of the ferries from Staten Island to Manhattan bears his name.

The Capodanno family had requested that a Mass be offered on board the ship; hence, after the commissioning ceremony, Chaplain James J. Killeen celebrated Mass in the vessel's small wardroom.

From the day of her commissioning, the *USS Capodanno* served the United States Navy and humanity well. As a part of Destroyer Squadron 12, the *USS Capodanno* was often deployed to the North Atlantic. During a deployment in the Summer of

1975, the ship was directly responsible for saving twenty-two lives in four rescue operations. One of the rescue operations took place off the southern coast of Italy and involved saving a ship-wrecked Italian family. After this deployment, the ship designation changed from a Destroyer Escort (DE-1093) to a Fast Frigate (FF-1093).

In February 1977, the *USS Capodanno* made her first visit to Staten Island. The ship docked at the Howland Hook Marine Terminal and was open for tours. Some 2,650 people visited the ship during her short stay in New York. During the stay, Pauline Costa invited the crew of the Capodanno to her home for dinner. After the meal, men of the ship's company entertained the family members with songs and stories of the ship. One song in particular made an impression on Pauline and she recorded it. It was about Father Vincent's abiding spirit within the ship and her crew. While the author of the song is unknown, the words to the song have been saved. The first verse is as follows:

The story's about a hero
A man of courage and fame
Vincent Capodanno,
That was the hero's name.

Capodanno was a man of God
Under the Vietnam sky.
His mission was to help mankind
And that is how he died.

Although he's gone
His memory lives on
All across the ocean
In a song.

If he could see
O how proud he would be
To have a ship in his name
And memory.

That's Capodanno
FF-1093.

In January 1979, the *USS Capodanno* was reassigned to Naval Surface Group FOUR and was home ported in Newport, Rhode Island, which is also the location of the Capodanno Memorial Chapel. The ship returned to the Staten Island area in May 1981. After the visit to the island, the ship was deployed to the Mediterranean and Black Seas. On September 4, 1981, the fourteenth anniversary of Father Vincent's death, the *USS Capodanno* received the first Papal blessing of any ship in the United States Fleet. Pope John Paul II blessed the *USS Capodanno* and her crew while they were docked in Naples, Italy.

There are many milestones in the life of a Navy ship. The keel laying, christening and commissioning ceremonies, and the changes of command all mark different points in her life. There is also a time for the final ceremony: the ship's decommissioning from active service. After 7,211 days of constant vigilance, the crew of the *USS Capodanno* hauled down the commissioning pennant and the entire crew came ashore.

Often the United States sells old ships to other countries. Hence, on July 30, 1993, the *USS Capodanno* was decommissioned from the United States Navy and transferred to the Turkish Navy. During the transferring ceremony, the ship was given her new name, *TCG Muavenet (F-250)*. The ship's bell is now at the Capodanno Memorial Chapel in Newport, Rhode Island.

In the Spring of 2000 Congressman Vito Fossella requested the Secretary of the Navy to consider naming a new Navy vessel after Father Capodanno. This effort, currently supported by 101 bipartisan House of Representatives, has received enthusiastic support. The petition stated "it is my hope to keep Lt. Capodanno's spirit and memory alive by naming a new destroyer in his honor."

THE INSPIRATION OF ART

Three major works of art have been created as memorials that solemnly depict the last moments of Father Vincent's life. The first is an oil painting by Douglas Rosa, and the second is a bronze statue by Antonio Pierotti. Another sculpture in memory of Father Vincent was created in Gaeta, Italy.

Before being commissioned by the Marine Corps to paint Vietnam battle scenes, Rosa had painted biblical scenes, especially passages from the Old Testament. To carry out his commission, Rosa particularly sought to portray the valor of Navy chaplains in Vietnam. He spoke with members of the Capodanno family to accurately render Father Vincent's physical build. He also interviewed the Marines who had been with Capodanno during the operation in which he lost his life.

Rosa commented, "The men told me just what happened — and the scene is right." He also took a helicopter to the actual spot in Vietnam so the background would be precise. The painting depicts the last and most memorable moment of Father Vincent as he kneels over the dying corpsman, desperately trying to lift him to safety as two other Marines nearby attempt to fight the battle. Rosa represents the chaplain's last moment as it really was: a struggle to save the life of a wounded brother while ignoring the personal cost.

The painting is presently displayed at the Chaplain School in Newport, Rhode Island. Chaplain Max A. Eller, past director of the Chaplain's School, described the painting and its impact on him:

> [The painting] is a beautiful, spectacular work of art. It so clearly dramatizes the sacrifice, the pathos, the heroic, the feet of clay of both Chaplains and Marines who face the perils of war while serving God and Country.

A second artistic representation of Father Vincent was commissioned by the Staten Island Marine Corps League, under the leadership of Gino Terranova, who wanted to memorialize Father Vincent in a unique way. A bronze statue, created in Carrera, Italy by Antonio Pierotti depicts the moment just before Father Vincent's death when he was kneeling over the dying corpsman — the same moment chosen for Rosa's painting. The scene is the same, but the perspectives are different. Rosa emphasizes the struggle and tension Father Vincent must have felt as he tried to rescue yet another Marine from a field of fire. In contrast, Pierotti accentuates the calm and prayerful attitude of Father Vincent. His face is peaceful, and he is able to hold an open book over the dying Marine. While Rosa's painting is most likely more accurate, Pierotti sought not only to exemplify the priest's last action, but also the many times he must have calmly knelt and prayed over a dying Marine in and out of combat.

After the work was completed, the five-ton statue was transported from Leghorn, Italy to Norfolk, Virginia on the *USNS Rigel*. From Norfolk the $15,000 statue was shipped to the Military Ocean Terminal in Bayonne, New Jersey.

On September 17, 1977, the statue was dedicated at the Army Chaplains School at Fort Wadsworth, on Staten Island. The Capodanno family attended the memorial Mass and dedication ceremony, along with Chaplain Stanley Beach and a few representatives from Maryknoll, including Fathers John Harrington and Peter Mullen. The Mass was celebrated by Bishop James J. Killeen, Auxiliary Bishop of New York and a former Navy chaplain. Pauline Costa had the honor of unveiling the life-size statue of her brother. While Fort Wadsworth is no longer used as the training school for Army chaplains, the statue still stands as a reminder to all of the countless acts of bravery this priest practiced daily while surrounded by death.

The last image of Father Vincent was fashioned in his father's birthplace in Gaeta, Italy. On February 24, 1990, a sculpture of Father Vincent Capodanno was unveiled in the town square which was newly renamed Piazza Capodanno. The Mayor of Gaeta invited the crew of the *USS Capodanno*, which was docked in Naples at the time, to the dedication ceremony of the new square and sculpture.

OTHER TRIBUTES

In various other ways, the legacy of Father Vincent Capodanno's life and death continues to inspire memorials and tributes.

On November 3, 1969, "Capodanno Hall" was dedicated at the San Francisco Bay Naval Shipyard. The hall serves as a Bachelor Officers' Quarters for eighty officers. Philip Capodanno was the only family member present for the dedication. Chaplain Herman J. Schnurr, Navy Captain and Roman Catholic priest, gave the address at the dedication. He noted how Father Vincent continued to preach a silent sermon:

To dedicate means to set aside as a monument, to establish a permanent object by which to preserve a living memory of this man, to serve as a constant example for all those naval officers who will pass this way. Even though he is now among the blessed, he continues to serve — because of the thoughts called forth by this reminder of his life.

On December 3, 1999, the Navy Personnel Research Studies and Technology Department in Millington, Tennessee, introduced its state of the art research facility named in honor of Father Vincent Capodanno. Frederick W. Smith, Chairman, President and CEO of Federal Express Corporation, who served with Father Capodanno in Vietnam, was the keynote speaker at the dedication ceremony.

A year later on December 1, 2000, in Gaeta, Italy, almost 100 years after Vincent Capodanno, Sr. emigrated from this port city, the Naval Support Activity honored his son. Their branch medical facility was named the Vincent Robert Capodanno Clinic.

On February 5, 1971, the Marine Corps Scholarship Foundation established the Chaplain Vincent R. Capodanno Memorial Scholarship to honor a fallen Marine and to give an opportunity for children of Marines to attend college. Two prominent supporters of this scholarship were also good friends of Father Vincent: Colonel Ed Fitzgerald, the main progenitor of the scholarship, and Chaplain Eli Takesian, the ranking chaplain of the Marine Corps in the mid-eighties. Takesian believes Father Vincent would have appreciated this memorial more than any other. He said:

> He believed strongly in and pushed strongly for his Marines. He would be absolutely delighted to know that scholarship aid, in his name, is being granted to deserving children of Marines.

In his hometown on Staten Island, on July 3, 1976, a stretch of Seaside Boulevard from Lily Pond Avenue to Elm Tree Avenue was renamed Father Capodanno Boulevard. After a memorial Mass at Holy Rosary Shrine in South Beach, Staten Island, a half-mile parade of Marines, Knights of Columbus and Boy

Scouts led the Capodanno family to the dedication site where both Congressman John M. Murphy and Colonel Ed Fitzgerald addressed the crowd gathered for the ceremony. During the event, family members unveiled an eight-foot-high Barre granite monument which told the story of Father Vincent's heroic act.

On November 15, 1975, one of the streets at the Newport Naval Education and Training Center, where the Navy Chaplains School is located, was named for Father Capodanno. Once again, the Navy remembered one of its own.

Four other major memorials, on which Father Capodanno's name appears, were built to commemorate not only his name but also representatives of various groups who gave their lives in the line of duty.

Two of the memorials are found at Freedoms Foundation in Valley Forge, Pennsylvania. The foundation was established to "contribute to the development of responsible citizens, encourage the practice of responsible citizenship, and to make Americans proud of America." Among the educational centers and many memorials at the Freedoms Foundation is the Medal of Honor Grove. The fifty-two-acre grove is divided into approximately one acre for each of the fifty states, Puerto Rico, and the District of Columbia, which contain the names of all 3,429 Medal recipients. The memorial area of the state of New York includes a seven-foot obelisk on which is mounted the state seal and a plaque listing all the Medal of Honor holders from that state. In July 1978, James Capodanno was present for the dedication of that memorial.

On October 6, 1979, the Capodanno family was once again present at the Freedoms Foundation for the dedication of a special obelisk displaying the names of the chaplains who received the Medal of Honor in recent wars. In both memorials, Father Vincent's name is fittingly among others who shared his extraordinary acts of valor.

Father Vincent Capodanno's name also appears on the Catholic Chaplains Memorial in Arlington National Cemetery. Among the eighty-three priests killed during the last three wars, seventy of them were from World War II, six from the Korean War, and seven from the Vietnam War. The priests came from forty-three dioceses and religious congregations, including Fathers Vincent Capodanno and William Cummings from Maryknoll.

The Chaplains Memorial was dedicated on May 21, 1989. More than 500 people, including James Capodanno, attended the memorial Mass celebrated by Archbishop Joseph Ryan of the Military Archdiocese. Mass was said at the National Cemetery's amphitheater and followed by the dedication ceremony on Chaplains' Hill. Father Vincent's brother together with the brother of Father Emil Kapaun, who died during the Korean War, unveiled the monument. Major General Patrick H. Brady, a Roman Catholic and a Medal of Honor recipient, spoke eloquently of the courage and sacrifice of the eighty-three priests:

> The chest of grace is inexhaustible because it comes from God. Not so the chest of freedom. It must continuously be replenished by our sacrifices. Today I think it is full. The great thing about these men is that they never really leave us. Dead or alive — the noblest part of their being stays with us; becomes a part of our being as people, in our military — everywhere in this great land, a part of our common ideals and feelings for each other, of all those things that make us a united country, a singular people, a people who enjoy each other's company and wish each other well.

Surely, the most profound and striking memorial to the 58,182 dead and missing soldiers from the Vietnam War is the Vietnam Memorial on the Mall in Washington, D.C. This memorial shows, like no other, the stark reality of war by listing every name of every man who either gave his life or was simply never found. Father Vincent had once said that the monument for those who were killed in battle should not be "of bronze or marble, but the living monument" of the good others had seen in them. However, monuments such as the Vietnam Memorial are enduring tributes which immortalize those who died serving their country and serve as a solemn reminder of the price our veterans paid for freedom.

On November 13, 1982, 150,000 gathered to dedicate the Vietnam Memorial, including Vincent's brother James and his sister Pauline. During the dedication speech, President Ronald Reagan mentioned the name of Father Vincent as one of the many who made the ultimate sacrifice. The names on the Wall are listed in chronological order: the first names listed were those of two advisers killed on July 6, 1959, and the last original name was that of Lieutenant Richard Vande Gier, who died on May 15, 1975. Father Vincent's name appears close to the middle of the Wall, specifically at panel 25E, line 95.

The Wall has been a source of healing for many who lost a relative, a friend, or a buddy in Vietnam. It is appropriate that Father Vincent Capodanno's name be immortalized in such a place of healing and consolation. During his final visit home, Father Vincent had to confront those who supported neither the war nor the veterans. In his last few months in Vietnam, he counseled and supported his men who had begun to sense the lack of support from their fellow Americans. In Father Vincent's letters to families of the wounded and dead Marines and by his constant presence with his men, he sought to be exactly what the Wall is — a source of healing and unification.

Sadly, many Vietnam veterans continue to be plagued by an aching wound that they were abandoned by their country, that their sacrifice a generation ago has gone unappreciated. But those who knew Father Vincent continue to fondly remember a holy man who did not abandon them. His sense of compassion, along with his extraordinary love and sacrifice for his Marines, are his legacy to them and to all of us.

POSTSCRIPT

The nation is finally seeking to understand the Vietnam War era and the sacrifices made by the hundreds of thousands of men and women who served there. For these veterans, unlike those of the past, the war continued in a painful and personal way far beyond their time of duty as they found themselves returning to a country which neither acknowledged nor appreciated their contribution. In some cases, the deepest convictions and motivations of these brave men and women were called into question.

Priests and ministers who served in Vietnam bore the burden of public criticism in a particular way. One of the saddest episodes in the protests against the Vietnam War was the criticism of these men of the cloth. Consider these lyrics of the popular 1968 song "Sky Pilot" sung by Eric Burden and the Animals:

He blesses the boys as they stand in line.
The smell of gun grease and their bayonets shine.
He's there to help them all that he can.
To make them feel wanted; he's a good holy man.

Sky pilot, sky pilot, how high can you fly?
You never, never, never reach the sky.

He smiles at the young soldiers, tells them it's all right.
He knows of their fear in the forthcoming fight.
Soon there'll be blood and many will die.
Mothers and fathers back home they will cry.

You mumble a prayer and it ends with a smile.
The order is given; they move down the line.
But he stays behind, and he'll meditate.
But it won't stop the bleeding or ease the hate.

And the young men move out into the battle zone.
He feels good; with God you're never alone.
He feels so tired and he lays [sic] on his bed.
Hopes the men will find courage in the words that he said . . .

In the morning they return with tears in their eyes.
The statue of death drips up to the skies.
A young soldier so ill looks at the sky pilot
Remembers the words 'Thou shalt not kill.'

It is clear that songs such as this one spring from a profound hatred of war and a desire for peace. At the same time, however, a stunning accusation is made about the wisdom and/or motivations of a military chaplain. Fortunately, in our time, the heroism and personal sacrifice of the chaplains who served in Vietnam is becoming better known and appreciated. This book hopes to contribute to the preservation of their memory.

Those who served in Southeast Asia, like their military forerunners, were flesh-and-blood human beings with the same set of complexities that we all share. Though he would be distinguished by the courageous manner of this death, Father Vincent Capodanno had very ordinary worries, concerns and hopes, many of which he carried only in his heart. There will always be a somewhat hidden and mysterious side of Father Vincent, as there is in all of us; there will always be questions about his life that can never be answered.

Still, while a complete understanding of his motivations remains unclear, there is no doubt that Father Vincent is a hero and an inspiration. True, he was killed while manifesting courage and sacrifice in the line of duty; but first and foremost his life was one of a dedicated priest who sought to realize that perfect charity to which we are all called. Ultimately, what should be remembered most about Father Vincent is not the way he died. His death was simply the last and greatest witness to what he believed and how he lived.

Despite the many justified memorials to his memory, perhaps the greatest tribute to Father Vincent Capodanno is his ability to still touch lives. One such example is recounted in the book *Maryknoll — At Work in the World*:

> A stranger walked into chapel last night, prayed devoutly for a while, then left. We asked him who he was and where he was from. He told us, then mentioned that he had been a teacher in the local high school during 1959–1960 and had known Father Capodanno who was here at that time. Then he went on to say that he had not been to church for several years, but after reading our article in the Catholic newspaper about Father Capodanno's death in Vietnam he decided it was time for him to get back to what the 'old' Church used to call his duties. . . . A missioner doesn't stop working even after he dies, does he?

A BIBLIOGRAPHIC ESSAY

This book came into existence after two years of research during which I had the good fortune to collect a large number of documents, letters, and personal accounts. Most of my documentation is original, and some sources will not be found in most libraries. I would like to provide here a list of these contacts and sources. I believe it will be helpful to some to know where I got my information and the wonderful resources available for people who want to do research, especially on the Vietnam War.

ORAL HISTORIES:

The most meaningful and important part of my documentation of the life of Father Vincent came from personal interviews I conducted with his family, fellow Maryknoll priests and those who served with him in Vietnam. In many cases it was no small task finding people who personally knew Father Vincent and were willing to share their story. Those who wish to hear these verbal histories would need to contact me directly through the publisher. I also have collected official documents and letters that offer insights into the life of Father Vincent. My interviews and documented sources include the following:

Family and Friends:
James Capodanno (brother)
Pauline Costa (sister)
Gloria Holman (sister)
Leon Thevenin (friend)
James Thomas (friend)

Maryknoll Priests
Rev. Paul Brien
Rev. Daniel Dolan
Rev. Donald McGinnis
Rev. John Rich
Rev. William Richter (a priest of the Diocese of Toledo, OH)
Rev. Donald Sheehan

Marines and Chaplains in Vietnam:
Captain Richard Alger (Intelligence Officer 7th Marines)
Chaplain Roy Baxter (Regimental Chaplain 7th Marines)
Chaplain Stanley Beach (Vietnam and Camp Pendleton)
Lieutenant Edward L. Blecksmith (2nd Platoon, M Company, 3/5)
Corporal David Brooks (2nd Platoon, M Company, 3/5)
Lieutenant Edward B. Burrow (B Company, 1/5)
Captain Thomas E. Byrne (Supply Officer 1st Engineer Battalion)
Sergeant Charles Carmin (D Company, 1/7)
Chaplain David Casazza (Chaplain 1st Marine Division)
Sergeant William L. DeLoach (1/7)
Major Ed Fitzgerald (XO 1/7)
Corporal Thomas Forgas (M Company, 3/5)
Corporal Bob Gerton (A Company 1/5)
Sergeant Thomas K. Gill (D Company, 1/5)
Captain Tony Grimm (Staff Officer 1/5)
Corporal James Hamfeldt (1/5)
Corporal Tim J. Hanley (I Company, 3/5)
Corporal Ray Harton (M Company, 3/5)
Corporal Henry Hernandez (Father Capodanno's Aide, 1/7)
Lieutenant Colonel Peter L. Hilgartner (CO 1/5)
Lieutenant Paul Hubble (USMC, Camp Pendleton)
Chaplain Richard Hunkins (Seabee Chaplain, Vietnam)
Captain Kenneth W. Johnson (M Company, 1/7)
Chaplain John Keeley (Division Chaplain)
Chaplain Charles T. Kelly (3/5)
Sergeant Richard L. Kline (M Company, 3/5)
Chaplain Victor Krulak (1st Medical Battalion)
Lieutenant Joseph L. LaHood (MD, 1st Medical Battalion)

Captain Raymond Leidich (CO A Company, 1/7)
PFC Stephen A. Lovejoy (M Company, 3/5)
Lieutenant Colonel Basile Lubka (CO 1/7)
Lieutenant Colonel Carl K. Mahakian (Vietnam)
Chaplain John J. O'Connor (Vietnam)
Thomas Panian (Vietnam)
Lieutenant Jerry G. Pendas (Operations Officer 1/7)
Corporal George Phillips (1st Platoon, M Company, 3/5)
Lieutenant Joseph E. Pilon (MD, 3/5)
Petty Officer George W. Reichert (Corpsman, 1st Medical Battalion)
PFC Julio Rodriquez (M Company, 3/5)
Corporal Keith J. Rounseville (M Company, 3/5)
Major Ray J. Savage (Communications Officer 1/7)
Corporal John Scafidi (K Company, 3/5)
Chaplain JD Shannon (Vietnam)
Lieutenant Frederick W. Smith (3/5)
Sergeant Grady Studdard (1/7)
Lieutenant Commander David Taft (MD, 1st Medical Battalion)
Chaplain Eli Takesian (5th Marine Chaplain)
Corporal Frederick W. Tancke (2nd Platoon, M Company, 3/5)
Corporal Joe Trischetti (2/11)
Colonel Gerald H. Turley (Logistics Officer, 7th Marines)
Captain David L. Walker (1/7)
Lieutenant Colonel Charles B. Webster (CO 3/5)
Captain Francis V. White (Operations Officer 3/7)
Chaplain Thomas J. Woolton (Vietnam)
Corporal Gerald D. Zimmerman (K Company, 3/5)

RESEARCH CENTERS:

THE MARINE CORPS HISTORICAL CENTER
Building 58
Washington Navy Yard
Washington, DC 20374
www.usmc.mil/historical.nsf/table+table+of+contents
The Marine Corps Historical Center is a gold mine of facts

and information on the history of the Corps. The Center exists to collect, record, preserve, exhibit and disseminate information about the Marine Corps. I obtained many details at the Center about the operations in which Father Vincent participated.

THE CHAPLAINS RESOURCE BOARD

6500 Hampton Blvd.

Norfolk, VA 23508-1296

www.chcnavy.org/index.htm

The Chaplains Resource Board (CRB) contains oral and written histories of the Navy Chaplain Corps. Father Vincent's original service record is kept at the CRB, as well as many other documents and pictures concerning his life and documentation on the many memorials that have been created since his death.

THE MARYKNOLL ARCHIVES

Maryknoll Fathers and Brothers

PO Box 304

Maryknoll, NY 10545-0304

www.maryknoll.org

The Maryknoll Archives maintain the seminary and missionary assignment records of Father Vincent Capodanno. The archives also keep the personal correspondence Father Vincent had with the Society, as well as a number of other documents and pictures.

BOOKS:

I found the following books to be of great help for background information about Maryknoll, the Chaplain Corps, and the Marines in Vietnam:

A Face of War, a film distributed by International Historic Films, Inc., 1985.

Bergsma, Herbert L., CMDR. *Chaplains with Marines in Vietnam 1962-1971*. Washington, D.C.: HQ, U.S. Marine Corps, 1985.

Clune, Frank. *Flight to Formosa*. London: Angus and Robertson Ltd., 1959.

Kittler, Glenn D. *The Maryknoll Fathers.* New York: World Publishing Company, 1961.

Marine Operations in Vietnam 1954-1973. Washington, D.C.: History & Museums Division, HQ, U.S. Marine Corps, 1985.

Michenfelder, Joseph F., M.M. *A Visit to Maryknoll.* Maryknoll, New York: Maryknoll Fathers, 1958.

Miller, Ed Mack. *Maryknoll—At Work in the World.* Maryknoll, New York: Maryknoll Fathers, 1974.

Moore, Withers M., CMDR. *Chaplains with U.S. Naval Units in Vietnam 1954-1975: Selected Experiences at Sea and Ashore.* Washington, D.C.: History Branch, Office of Chief of Chaplains, Department of the Navy.

Murphy, Edward F. *Vietnam Medal of Honor Heroes.* New York: Ballantine Books, 1987.

Nevins, Albert J. *The Meaning of Maryknoll.* New York: McMullen Books, 1954.

Passero, Ernest F. "For God, Corps, and Country." *Marine Corps Gazette 69,* #10, October, 1985.

Plus, Raoul, S.J. *Radiating Christ: An Appeal to Militant Catholics.* London: Burns, Oates and Washbourne Ltd., 1936.

Shulimson, Jack. *U.S. Marines in Vietnam An Expanding War 1966.* Washington, D.C.: HQ, U.S. Marine Corps, 1982.

Shulimson, Jack and Johnson, Charles M., Major *Marines in Vietnam The Landing and the Buildup 1956.* Washington, D.C.: HQ, U.S. Marine Corps, 1978.

Surface, Bill and Hart, Jim. *Freedom Bridge: Maryknoll in Hong Kong.* New York: Coward-McCann, Inc., 1963.

Telfer, Gary L., Major, Rogers, Lane, Lieutenant Colonel, and Fleming, V. Keith, Jr. *U.S. Marines in Vietnam Fighting the North Vietnamese 1967.* Washington, D.C.: HQ, U.S. Marine Corps, 1984.

Walsh, James E., M.M., D.D. *Maryknoll Spiritual Directory.* New York: Field Afar Press, 1947.

Wiest, Jean-Paul. *Maryknoll In China, A History, 1918-1955.* Armonk, New York: M.E. Sharpe, Inc., 1988.

Vincent Capodanno
Eighth grade graduation picture from Public School 44, Staten Island, NY 1947.
Photograph courtesy of Curtis High School

Father Vincent with Mother (Rachel)
Ordination day: June 14, 1958
Courtesy of The Estate of Mrs. Pauline Costa

1958
Front row from left; Eleanor, Dorthy, Rachel (Mom).
Back row from left; Jim, Marie(Mary), Philip, Albert,
Gloria, Father Vincent, Pauline.
Courtesy of Mr. James Capodanno

Maryknoll World Headquarters and Training Center for the Catholic Foreign Mission Society of America, Maryknoll, New York

Fr. Capodanno's graduation picture from the Maryknoll Seminary. 1958

The Departure Bell is rung once a year during the Sending Ceremony of Maryknoll Missions to Asia, Africa, and Latin America.
Courtesy of The Catholic Foreign Mission Society.

Father Vincent going up for his mission crucifix at the departure ceremony on Sunday, June 15, 1958.
Courtesy of The Estate of Mrs. Pauline Costa

Father Vincent saying Mass as a missionary in Taiwan.
Courtesy of The Estate of Mrs. Pauline Costa

Father Vincent with the School Children in Taiwan in his missionary church.
Oct 1962
Courtesy of Pauline Costa

Father Vincent being sworn in as a Navy Lieutenant of the Chaplain Corps. on Dec 28, 1965 by Commander E.M. Tollgaard in Honolulu, Hawaii.
Courtesy of United States Navy Chaplain Resource Board, Norfolk, VA

Father Vincent, newly inducted as Lieutenant, in the United States Navy, attends a briefing in January, 1966.
Courtesy of United States Navy Chaplain Resource Board, Norfolk, VA

The Catholic church at Fuc Wa, S.Vietnam, 1966.
Courtesy of Chaplain Roy Baxter

Father Vincent leading a field prayer service for the grunt Marines of the 1st Batallion, 7th Marines in the Muo Douc area, Vietnam, September 11, 1966. *Courtesy of the Navy Chaplain Resource Board, Norfolk, VA*

The exterior and interior of the Chapel of Chu Lai which was built for Father Vincent by the grunts of the 1st Battalion, 7th Marines.
Courtesy of 1st Sergeant Charles L. Carmin, USMC (Ret.)

The President of the United States takes pride in presenting the
BRONZE STAR MEDAL (posthumously) to

LIEUTENANT VINCENT R. CAPODANNO
CHAPLAIN CORPS
UNITED STATES NAVAL RESERVE

for service as set forth in the following

CITATION:

For heroic achievement in connection with operations against the enemy while serving as Chaplain, 1st Battalion, 7th Marines, United States Marine Forces in the Republic of Vietnam from May to December 1966. Lieutenant Capodanno participated in Operations MOBILE, FRANKLIN, FRESNO, GOLDEN FLEECE 7-1, and RIO BLANCO. He repeatedly and purposely accompanied those forces most likely to experience the greatest enemy contact. Frequently, he unhesitatingly exposed himself to intense enemy fire as he moved across open areas to assist Marines who needed his help and prayer. On more than one occasion, Lieutenant Capodanno administered first aid while under fire and moved wounded Marines to secure areas to comfort them until medical assistance could be obtained. During Operation RIO BLANCO, with complete disregard for his own safety, Lieutenant Capodanno, repeatedly exposed himself while he moved throughout the positions, encouraging and inspiring the men during intense enemy fire. He inspired confidence in the Marines and contributed immeasurably to the successful accomplishment of the unit's mission. In addition to his performance on the battlefield, Lieutenant Capodanno served as an example and loyal friend to the officers and men of the battalion. He worked long into the night to counsel and serve the men, write to their parents, and assist them with their problems. His fair, but firm, approach to the problems common to a combat area won the deep respect of the battalion personnel. Lieutenant Capodanno's courageous actions, initiative, and complete dedication to duty reflected great credit upon himself and were in keeping with the highest traditions of the United States Naval Service.

The Combat Distinguishing Device is authorized.

For the President,

Commandant of the Marine Corps

190

Chaplain (Lt.) Vincent
Capodanno was awarded
the Medal of Honor post-
humously after he was
killed by intense machine-
gun fire while aiding
others in Vietnam.

Capodanno Chapel, Iwakuni, Japan, was dedicated to
Father Vincent Capodanno.
Courtesy Chaplain Resource Board, Norfolk, VA

St. Vincent Chapel, Taiwan, was dedicated to the
Memory of Father Vincent Capodanno.
Courtesy of Rev. Daniel Dolan, MM

The dramatic statue honoring Father Capodanno's service at Fort Wadsworth, Staten Island, New York. *Courtesy of Susan Weber*

The *USS Capodanno:* Keel Laid February 25.1972. Christened on October 21, 1972.
Commission Date November 17, 1973.

Douglas Rosa in front of his painting of Father Vincent ministering to Marines in the fields of Vietnam.
Courtesy of Chaplain Resource Board, Norfolk, VA

The Congressional Medal of Honor awarded on January 7, 1969 to Mr. James Capodanno by Paul R. Ignatius, Secretary of the Navy. They are joined here by Father Capodanno's nephew, James, who is in the Army.

Phillip Capodanno (center) unveils the Dedication Plaque at the Capodanno Hall, San Francisco Bay Naval Shipyard, California, November 3, 1969.
Courtesy of The Chaplain Resource Board, Norfolk, VA

The Vietnam War Memorial Wall, Washington, DC

VINCENT R CAPODANNO

Panel 25E—Line 95

Items clockwise from left: Fr. Capodanno's dog tags, Naval Officer shield from his Officer's cover, Ships emblem of USS Capodanno, Painting of Fr. Capodanno on the battle field, Service Ribbons awarded to Fr. Capodanno during his eighteen months in Vietnam.

Courtesy of The United States Naval Chaplain's School, Newport, RI

The Reverend Vincent Robert Capodanno Foundation

The Reverend Vincent Robert Capodanno Foundation is a non-profit organization under the laws of the State of Virginia. The purpose of the Foundation is to spread the message of Christ as it was exemplified in the life, work and death of Fr. Vincent. The Foundation continues the work of Fr. Vincent, dedicating its programs of ministry to veterans and people in the armed forces.

For more information about the Foundation, you are invited to contact the Foundation by writing:

The Reverend Vincent Robert Capodanno Foundation, Inc.
9716 Banting Drive
Fairfax, Virginia 22032
(703) 503-3489
e:mail — info@Father-Capodanno.org

You are also invited to visit the Foundation website, which features a photo gallery, stories about Fr. Vincent, a newsletter and events calendar, as well as a forum for discussion and opportunities to share with others your own stories about Fr. Vincent.

http://www.father-capodanno.org

INDEX

To order additional copies of this book:

Please complete the form below and send for each copy

CMJ Marian Publishers
P.O. Box 661 • Oak Lawn, IL 60454
toll free 888-636-6799
call 708-636-2995 or fax 708-636-2855

email jwby@aol.com
www.cmjbooks.com

Name _____

Address _____

City _____ State ____ Zip _____

Phone (   ) _____

	QUANTITY	SUBTOTAL

The Grunt Padre(hardcover)
         $ 22.95 each   x _____   = $ _____

The Grunt Padre(softcover)
         $15.95 each   x _____   = $ _____

Radiating Christ
         $10.00 each   x _____   = $ _____

Becoming the Handmaid of the Lord
         $13.75 each   x _____   = $ _____

Our Lady of the Outfield
         $10.95 each   x _____   = $ _____

Seeking Christ in The Crosses
    and Joys of Aging
         $12.95 each   x _____   = $ _____

Though I Walk Through the Valley
         $14.95 each   x _____   = $ _____

Sacraments The Masterworks of God
         $ 5.95 each   x _____   = $ _____

Before The Altar
         $12.00 each   x _____   = $ _____

           + tax (for Illinois residents only)   = $ _____

                   + 15% for S & H   = $ _____

                      TOTAL   = $ _____

☐ Check # _____ ☐ Visa ☐ MasterCard   Exp. Date ___/___/___

Card # _____

Signature _____